Your Other Half

Your Other Half

the guide to better relationships with others & yourself

Sophie Personne

ISBN 13 - 9781540452832
ISBN - 1540452832
Library of Congress Control Number: 2016919694
CreateSpace Independent Publishing Platform
North Charleston, South Carolina

Contents

Acknowledgements

This is probably the hardest part of the book to write. Numerous people have knowingly or unknowingly contributed, just by being a part of my life at some point or another and allowing me to learn through their experiences or turmoil.

I particularly want to thank my uncle, Jacques Billard, for illustrating the book at very short notice indeed (sorry...) and helping me to 'draw a concept'.

I am very lucky to have been supported by many people over the years. I couldn't start to name everyone so I just want to say thank you to you all, not just for your encouragement but for simply being there for me.

Sophie

Testimonials

'I loved it! Not only is it a good read, it makes so much sense. Why haven't I seen this stuff before!' – *Cindy Coe, Southampton, UK*

'Sophie is very wise and her words really resonate with me. I didn't even realise I had a problem to start off with, I just thought I could improve things a bit. The fact she looks at things in such a different way and explains it all in a no non-sense way has made so much difference in my life and has helped me to get the results I always wanted. Simply brilliant!' - *Dan Nyhan, Weston-Super-Mare, UK*

'I could actually discuss your book with you all day, because I love all this psychology stuff. Well done ☺ Good job. I enjoyed the book, it was thought provoking and I think it will help people.' – *Michelle Pentland, Southampton, UK*

'I LOVED IT! Well worth a read and now I want to go back and read it again. Or even part 2? I can see why your book is going to be popular, because it is so honest.' – *Bronwen Vearncombe, Meon Valley, UK*

'The way Sophie looks at situations and explains the way people behave has really helped me to see things in a different light and has brought me to look at the way I communicate, not just with others, but with myself too.

I have learnt to see and understand the way people act and how I can react to it, change the way I come across as well as my own behaviour so that I can get better results in the way I communicate with others.' – *Claire P, Paris, France*

'Sophie blew me away to be honest. She is very wise and can see spot the real problems very quickly and accurately. The way she explains things and makes sense of it all, well, there are no words for it. After all these years of making the same mistakes again and again, now I understand why and I am clear on what I need to do next and how. When you talk to your friends or family, they give you their opinions about what you should do and that doesn't help. Sophie looks at it completely differently and I am very grateful, this will change the rest of my life for the better.' – *D.W., Southampton, UK*

'I really enjoyed reading your book, indeed so much so I read it twice in 2 days!! :) I know having read that accepting compliments may be difficult for you, but I reckon you are going to have to get used to that, as I am sure that I will not be the only person impressed by what you have written!

I really enjoyed your writing style which I found to be conversational and relaxed, yet professional. It felt to me that through your words you were talking to me like you would a client. I therefore found it easier to read and relate to which was important as some of the content contained some tough messages and truths. As you can tell this really resonated with me, because what you wrote impacted and influenced me personally, making me think differently about how I view the world around me.

In my view, anyone reading this book who has current relationship issues or wants explanation to past relationship difficulties, will begin to find the means to deal with them through your book.

Sophie, you can be justifiably proud of what you have created with your book. Please do not stop here; I believe that you have other books within you to write. Great job, very well done.' – *Philip Gale, Felpham, UK*

1

Introduction

The world constantly evolves and it's fair to say that since the second World War, we have seen some of the most amazing technological advances, especially in terms of communication. The way we interact with each other, and on a global level, has been totally revolutionised. Very few people could 'survive' without the internet today and a large number of us have become surgically attached to our phones.

The last 20 years have totally changed the world. The way we live, do business, work or even buy things is totally different. Everything is pretty much instant and at the touch of a button. How we meet people, act, develop relationships and interact with others has been dramatically transformed.

The internet provides us with various means to keep in touch, in a manner that a simple phone line could not do. The opportunities are now worldwide, allowing us to travel around the globe and experience new cultures thanks to the advent of cheap airlines, but also from the depths of our settees. Let's not forget that only 50 years ago, most people never went abroad and normally stayed fairly close to their roots. Few of us would even venture very far once we had flown the nest.

Today, we have the world quite literally at our fingertips and we are the most connected we have ever been. We are also probably the loneliest.

It seems odd how this could be the case when we have access to people on a global level at any point of day or night. But it is the case. We are actually disconnected. Just go anywhere, anytime, and notice how people who are obviously out together, will check their phones. The world around them has disappeared. Literally, just like that... and you'll struggle to get an answer out of them until they re-emerge. If you keep watching, the next thing you'll see is people getting their phone out to take pictures, which will then be uploaded to Facebook (or any other social media platform for that matter), so that other people across the street can feel the need to check their mobiles and vacate reality for a moment. Now it's on Facebook, the world can see how much of a good time they're having.

But are they really? So much time is now spent taking the right photo, uploading it, then going back to the phone to check how many likes we got or what urgent comments we need to respond to... Time that we would otherwise have dedicated to the people who we are actually out with. To be fair, a lot of us are guilty of doing that. We just need to know what's happened in the last 5 minutes or what that last message was about.

This really shows the actual disconnection we are currently experiencing, not only with other people but with ourselves. We are no longer aligned with what we really want or need, but more with what we perceive the world to expect of us, and what we feel we ought to do. This isn't even a conscious decision that we are making, it is the new unconscious peer pressure, which is completely different from what it used to be. There is the clear social anxiety of losing out. Firstly, an obvious example: if you haven't got a Facebook account, you are out of it, aren't you? You won't see the updated photos or easily find out about what's going on in people's lives. It would take effort to keep in touch with what they have been up to. So if you can't beat them, join them hey? There is actually a second element to this fear of missing out and it is about life. We compare our own to others… and that can make us feel pretty inadequate, especially in a world of having it all, now.

It's all a bit grim really when you start looking at the current reality. What hope have we got?

Well, we do. And this book wants to show you exactly the problems that you are facing, so they can be more easily recognisable, and then explain to you how a simple shift in the way you look at things can transform your life. It will also assist you with understanding the real deep root cause. We often think that we know what that is but we can be very misguided, as what we see as problems are actually merely symptoms of the real issue. I will then explain to you how you can start to address some of what you are currently experiencing in your life and how some easy little steps can make all the difference.

The ultimate benefits of this book are that you will not only understand how the new world dynamics are working, but also to become more aware of your own place in that world. It will give you tools to learn how you can be happy in your own skin, whilst interacting with others better, being comfortable with your own decisions and self-reliant.

2

Setting The Scene

*F*irst things first… You may or may not be familiar with Neuro Linguistic Programming (otherwise known as NLP) but as you'll find a number of references to it throughout the book, it is worth explaining a bit more about it before we move on.

So what's NLP?

It is a set of tools and techniques which were developed in the seventies by Richard Bandler and John Grinder, for the purpose of better communication and personal development. It can easily be explained like so:

- Neuro - the mind
- Linguistic - words & body language
- Programming - patterns of behaviours learnt and repeated

Basically, it is a method to understand yourself, why you act and react as you do or what makes you tick. The set of techniques used are to help you change and influence your own behaviour, utilising language and other types of communication in order for you to create new, more helpful, ways of being.

It is a means to change the responses that don't serve you so you can start getting what you want instead. This approach shows how our assumptions affect our behaviours, actions and results in life. It addresses the consequences of what we have brought to ourselves.

NLP will also teach you how to communicate better, not just with other people, but within yourself. Our very own internal self-dialogue and patterns of thought can sometimes be quite damaging and a few simple tweaks often make a world of difference.

The importance of relationships

So we obviously all know that relationships are important and it goes without saying really... But do we really understand why? And why, actually, they are at the core of everything?

The common sense of the word is often subconsciously associated with love and partnerships. We sometimes forget that we have relationships with just about everyone and anyone we come into contact with (including those people we don't even like or are indifferent to).

Our state of mind is more often than not affected by our relations and interactions with others, whether positive or negative. If we take a road rage incident for example, you most probably don't know the other driver but their actions and the impact they will have on you have the power to change your day and the way you feel. For the briefest of moments, there was a relationship between both parties. We wouldn't even think of it really at a conscious level because we don't know the person. The interaction however created something, a reaction which has the potential to create a chain of events.

The Butterfly Effect

Have you ever heard how a butterfly taking off and using his wings to fly can create a storm on the other side of the world? I actually struggled with that concept at the beginning of my journey because I couldn't quite see (or remotely understand) how such a tiny insignificant act could have such an impact and result in such an outcome. It was my NLP trainer who actually explained it in the best way at the time, by giving me an example of something that had happened to her.

This was something that could happen to anyone on any given day. She was on the motorway and had overtaken a car just before a toll. However, as she was getting back into the lane, the traffic came to a halt, so in effect, she pretty much cut the guy up. He was obviously not impressed by that and she could see him swearing and gesturing in all manners that weren't necessarily pleasant. She tried to raise her hand to say sorry but at that point, could see it did very little.

The impact of that single interaction could have repercussions that we don't even think about. The man was in such a state and extremely angry. The queue at the toll was probably not helping matters either and it was quite probable that his full attention would not be on the road once he had gone through the toll. What would be on his mind would be things like 'I can't believe how this woman cut me up!', 'do people not know how to drive?!?!' and so on... You get the idea. In essence, because the man's attention isn't on the road, there is a fairly high probability that he could in turn cause an accident, which could have devastating consequences, including death. The road closures to investigate the causes of the crash and subsequent traffic delays could have further effects on other people's lives and their moods or levels of tiredness, which could lead to more accidents, missing out on their child's nativity play, etc. The ripples are endless and of various levels of importance but only started because of something insignificant in itself.

In this particular instance, she explained at the toll what had happened and said she would pay for the car behind too, also asking the attendant to apologise on her behalf. The other car actually caught up with her and smiled with his thumb up. The negative aspect of her actions was turned into a positive one.

Everything we do or say has an impact but we don't always realise that, especially if the effect is felt down the line by someone we don't even know.

What is the correlation between relationships and NLP?

In Neuro-Linguistic Programming, there are a number of presuppositions that we work with and believe to be true. I will explain more about some of those as we go through and as they become relevant. The first one I'd like to mention is that 'we cannot *not* communicate', as I see it intrinsically linked to the butterfly effect and the ripples it produces. Communication is the basis of all relationships.

First of all, I will remind you that it isn't just about what we say. In fact, the words we use only represent 7% of the way we communicate. 38% is about the delivery and the tone of voice that we use whilst 55% is body language. So if you're really grumpy and tell someone that you're fine and just dandy, that person will get the vibe that something isn't adding up. The actual meaning of your words won't be in sync with the way you are saying it, your physiology and it will feel incongruent.

The reason why I am mentioning this now is to set the scene.

Whether it's face to face, by phone, text or email, the way you say things or your mood transpires and what you do or don't do will be perceived in a certain way. Let me give you a personal example. I suffered a nervous breakdown and as I didn't want to take tablets, I decided I would coach myself back to health. At the time, very few people knew it had happened and I intended on keeping it that way. I didn't really want to see or speak to anybody, I just wanted to be left alone so I could sort myself out. I am normally quite an extrovert but I felt I needed to withdraw from social occasions, as I was really struggling when I was around other people. The energy required to put and keep the mask on was killing me inside. So I stopped going and made fairly valid excuses (in my mind anyway). I also withdrew from being as active as I used to be on Facebook and whilst I wasn't someone who posted a status update every 5 minutes, I had a regular pattern. Within no time at all, I was frequently asked by people, even random ones who hardly knew me, if I was ok. From my lack of engagement and tone, they had unconsciously worked out something was wrong.

Relationships are at the core of everything

As I have just demonstrated, the way we interact amongst ourselves has a major impact on our lives and happiness. Very few people can actually survive on their own for a long time, as we all need to have some form of contact with others to survive. This is why prisons use solitary confinement as a form of punishment.

Even individuals who don't necessarily like to be around people will have more relationships than they realise. First of all, through work. They may not have many friends but they will have some. They may not have a family but they more than likely will have neighbours, and whilst they may not necessarily realise it, they actually still rely on others and aren't totally alone.

I actually have an interesting fact that confirms our relations are the most essential part of our lives. I was told only recently by a friend of mine who is a psychic medium and tarot reader, that 90% of her customers come to ask a question about relationships, which is a massive number. They are either singletons wanting to meet someone or wondering if the person they've met is right for them, troubled marriages, problems with parents, kids, colleagues, ... (non-exhaustive list). When I asked her what the second most commonly asked question was, it surprised me. I believed it might be relating to careers and work, but it isn't. It's about moving house - I know this doesn't relate to relationships but I thought I'd share it with you anyway.

The grim reality

Love is something that is pretty much top of the list for most people and that is sought by many. Whether you are in a relationship, married or single and struggling to meet someone, if things aren't going your way in that department, it really is going to affect your levels of happiness.

A simple Google search returned some frightening statistics:

- In 2013, there were 114,720 divorces in England and Wales. The highest level of divorce for men and women is between the ages of 40 and 44. The number of divorces is decreasing as people are now cohabitating more. *(Source - ONS)*
- 'Current bank account' relationship average is 17 years and marriage average is 11 years 6 months. *(Source - BBC News)*
- 42% of marriages end in divorce. *(Source - ONS)*
- 1/5 of UK couples are close to break up. (Relate study) – May 2016 *(Source - BBC News)*
- Population aged 16 and over who were single increased from 29.6% in 2002 to 34.5% in 2015. - *(Source - ONS)*
- Population aged 16 and over who were living in a couple was 60.5 % in 2015. - *(Source - ONS)*
- 4-10% of people in England will experience depression in their life time. *(Source – **www.mentalhealth.org.uk**)*

The picture it depicts isn't great to be honest and I think the majority of us would like to just meet the right person and settle without any major disruptions for the rest of our lives. From the facts above, it clearly isn't the case though.

So is this it then?

Well, I'd like to think that it isn't. This is actually why I decided to write this book, because I genuinely believe it doesn't have to be. It is only this way because people just aren't aware of some very simple concepts and ideas that can change their lives once they understand and apply them.

I have spent a number of years watching and researching people. I guess it started when I was put in charge of staff because understanding why on earth they would do certain things was important and also beyond me... As time went on, I became genuinely interested in finding out what makes us tick, why and how we make the decisions that we do, why we act like we do, our motivations and also, the different reactions we can have in different circumstances or environments. The human mind is truly extraordinary and it is really interesting to study how our upbringing and beliefs shape us, as well as the power of habits and comfort. Whilst it is impossible to predict what someone will do next, it is more than possible to understand different types of people and where they are coming from.

My background is managerial and for my sins, I spent most of my early career in the security industry. I was pretty much the only woman in a world full of men and I learnt pretty quickly that to survive, not saying boo to a goose really wasn't the way forward. It was a fairly close environment, with the biggest variety of characters and personalities, which led to a number of clashes and confrontations. As 'the female', I became the person they would go to for a chat. Their problems ranged from single people dating and getting it wrong, affairs and how they were justified, deeply unhappy marriages and not knowing what to do about it, lack of a sex life or whatever else they would come and surprise me with. I remember the lengths of efforts some were going to in trying to hide an affair, i.e. a guy pretending to have been night fishing and coming back to the office, rolling around in puddles whilst actually wiping himself with a fresh fish he had just bought from the shop. To be honest, if he had put as much effort in confronting the marital issues, he may well have been able to solve them!

One of the major things I realised was the impact relationships in general were having on all of these people's lives, and actually, on mine too. I worked out that if I could help them at home so to speak, and improve their lives there, my life would be a lot easier, because there would be less 'sickness', less turnover, less customer complaints (therefore less disciplinaries) and less customer terminations. In a nutshell, the work performance was so closely related to the home situation that the aggravation levels dropped dramatically. Even for those who were throwing themselves into work because they weren't happy at home, I noticed an improvement on their concentration levels and performance once the issues had been resolved.

After retraining in Neuro Linguistic Programming, which is after all the science of communication which is in turn the basis of all relationships, I started to understand the complexities a lot better. To get it right, there are other elements (such as mindset for instance) that we will discuss in greater detail later on. Once I had identified them, it became fairly easy from the onset, to spot who was going to be successful and who wasn't. Certain traits were beginning to appear consistently and over the years, I started to understand how this could all work together.

So why now?

I have previously briefly mentioned it but the nervous breakdown was probably what changed everything for me. Whilst I wouldn't go back through it in a hurry, I also totally understand why it happened and how it has changed me for the better. I was so adamant I would not take medication but yet I was so unwell, I had no other choice but to seriously look at myself and my life. I had previously been close to one a few years ago, so there had to be patterns of thought and behaviours or self-beliefs at play there. I had to find the deeper reasons, as opposed to what anyone would have put it down to, if I wanted to sort myself out once and for all.

It is fairly uncomfortable to face your own home truths. But all of a sudden, I got it, I just literally had an epiphany, which I could not have had without going through the process and the pain. It's a bit like when they say that you can't run before you walk, you can't get to the bottom of things just like that, you have to do the work.

Once I had found the answer I was looking for, I also realised that it actually wasn't just about me, but that anyone could do it. One of the NLP techniques that is taught is called 'modelling'. Basically, you find someone who is the best at what they are doing, study the way they do it, copy the exact method and apply it to your own life. So I started using my own technique in my coaching work, and soon enough, everything was falling into place. All of those who applied the process and genuinely did the work got results. Those who weren't ready or willing, didn't.

So this is why I am writing this now. I want to make a difference in people's lives and to a degree, change the world we live in by motivating people to understand themselves, grow and as a result, be happy. Not just within themselves but with others, so they can create positive and long lasting relationships with realistic 'expectations'.

The aim of this book is to get you on your way and give you the foundations of an authentic happy life, whilst being true to who you are, learn how to communicate better and understand others.

3

Your Current Problems

Whilst what you will read below would relate to all relationships, we will focus here more on romantic connections and partnerships, whether you are single and struggling to meet someone or currently attached and wanting to improve the state of affairs. What we experience in either of these situations is normally pretty similar in terms of the frustrations and angst, however, the pain points are slightly different, which is why I have created 2 different 'Symptoms Sheets'. You can download them at **www.sophiepersonne.com/your-other-half-downloads/**. It is a fairly straight forward exercise, which will allow you to pinpoint exactly what bothers you the most. Whilst it will state the obvious, the idea is that you are tracing a line in the sand and will be able to get back to it later on to remind yourself of progress.

So, whether you are feeling hopeless in your quest for love or just don't know what to do anymore to sort things out, in both cases, it is probably fair to say that the following statements will describe your feelings quite accurately:

- Stuck in a rut
- Powerless
- Not as happy as you could be
- Settling for a life that you don't really want
- Wondering if it will change
- Worried that life is passing you by

You are probably carrying this weight completely on your own and with little support. It is easy to think back to happier times, wondering where it actually all went wrong and wish you could feel what it's like at the beginning again.

Falling in love and how it affects us

Falling in love is possibly one of the best feelings in the world and one of the most exhilarating things anyone could ever experience. Nothing can prepare us for it as it is often quite sudden and comes as a surprise. It normally hits us when we least expect it.

Unfortunately, falling in love is also one of the worst feelings in the world. The emotional and physiological instability it brings can be overwhelming or difficult to deal with, as we wrestle with the highs and lows of our emotions.

This is caused by all the chemicals it releases on the brain, which actually reacts in exactly the same way it would if we were on drugs. Our levels of dopamine increase, which has the same effect as taking cocaine, and the reason why we don't seem to be able to concentrate on anything. Our levels of serotonin decrease and this normally leads to some form of obsessive behaviour, like checking our phones every 30 seconds. We literally become lost and our mind struggles to focus on anything but the object of our desires.

Most of us will have experienced the emotional rollercoaster it sends us on, from the butterflies in the stomach, the lack of sleep to the loss of appetite. When we fall in love with somebody, it feels that life will never be the same again. We become emotionally dependent on that person, continually wanting to please them and make them happy. The thought of being without them is unbearable and we can also become very possessive of them.

It is quite easy to know whether the feeling is reciprocated and there are many self-help books or articles on the subject. We want to reassure ourselves that the emotions are both ways and will look out for just about any signs. As human beings, we often over-analyse, especially as we become more and more aware that we could get very hurt if the other person didn't feel the same way so we seek reassurance.

There are actually 3 stages to falling in love.

The first one is pure lust. Basically, it's the initial appeal and chemistry. Let's not forget that despite evolution, we are still animals and react as such, essentially driven by our hormones. Incidentally, this chemistry reaction happens in all relationships, which is why you will be drawn to certain people and choose their friendships for instance but not others.

The second stage is the attraction phase where we quite literally lose ourselves to our feelings. We just cannot get enough of that person and are totally love struck. This part can't last for too long because our brain is completely messed up and we pretty much lose our ability to function. This is actually the foundation for the rest of the relationship. Research has also shown that the attraction phase will last longer if there are any physical or social barriers, mainly because it becomes a very conscious choice to be together as opposed to just taking it as it comes.

The third stage is the attachment period. This is the time when people truly create the bond that will keep them together and it is the precursor to a longer lasting commitment. It has been found that when people have to go through some form of adversity together, their feelings intensify quite significantly.

Nothing can prepare us for the emotions we experience when we fall in love. We can try and stay as grounded as possible but the whirlwind will take over.

When it goes wrong

Unfortunately, not all relationships will work nor can they all be saved, as the time spent ignoring the issues can be extremely damaging in the long run. When you find yourself wondering if it is time to leave, it's not generally good news.

This is a conclusion that may take years to reach and highlights issues that may have been lingering for a very long time. Sometimes, people actually don't have the guts to confront the situation and leave. They feel that the process is just too difficult and don't want to have to face the consequences their decision will bring. There is often an element of guilt too, the sense that things should have worked out, hence the common 'It's not you, it's me'. And actually, the problem comes from both parties, it's just that only one of them has identified it and is doing something about it, which makes them feel bad.

Obviously, this is a general overview, and each situation will have its own particular characteristics, but on the whole, some of the principles below will apply to all.

To put it bluntly, if you are unhappy in a relationship, unless you decide to tackle the issues, you are unlikely to lead a happy life and will grow to resent each other. End of. So it is far better to be honest with yourself and face the situation.

First of all, it's important to establish what's not working anymore as opposed to just voicing unhelpful generalisations. Some of what you see as a problem might actually be a response to your own behaviour. Your partner may not even realise they are doing something that you are deeply unhappy about.

Whichever way this is going to go, you need to talk. Yes, it's obvious but you would be amazed how many people skip that important step. They will assume they know what the other has to say and have the conversations in their own heads, but never actually sit somebody down and tell them they are unhappy. And that's purely because they don't want to upset the balance. 'Maybe it's just me? I'll try and work it out myself' is a very common statement and something I hear regularly.

Unfortunately, what people don't realise, is that the moment they do that, they have actually started the grieving process. They will go through all of the emotions associated with the loss of a relationship without even realising it. This is why the decision to leave often comes as a shock for the partner who was totally oblivious to what was going on. The person leaving the relationship will be seen to move on too quickly, leading to all sorts of assumptions that they must have been cheating and it often couldn't be further from the truth. It's just that their grieving started a long time ago, and as they reach their decision, complete the process.

In most cases, just the pure fact of asking yourself if you should leave is the beginning of a downwards spiral, and indicates that the issues are deeply rooted. Trying to work at them without voicing the fact you are doing so often leads to only one outcome.

The best way is to be honest with your partner. They deserve it and so do you. Burying your head in the sand will just make it all the more painful and complicated. Quite simply, it isn't fair on anyone and staying in an unhappy relationship eventually leads to more hurt for all involved.

Remember that commitment, whether you are married or not, takes some work from both parties. The vows that you take or the mortgage that you sign together are only the beginning of the journey. The key is to 'renew those vows' on a daily basis, not let routine take over but especially not take the other person for granted. It all seems so obvious but it is easily done, and we all need to be reminded regularly so we don't end up in a situation where we have to ask ourselves, 'is it time to leave'?

It doesn't have to be the only conclusion that you come to though, but it's worth bearing in mind that it is ok to do so if the relationship has run its course.

A difficult place to be

So, whether you are now single or in an unhappy relationship wondering what to do next, let's be realistic, it's not the best of times. And yes, I know that some people are happy single and don't want to meet anybody but then I doubt they are reading this book. I also know some people would actually prefer to stay in a relationship that doesn't bring them anything rather than being on their own. What I am talking about here, it's those of you who are dissatisfied and want more from life.

It can be a very painful process to go through, especially as we don't always feel we can talk about it. We don't always want to burden others and we know that there are other people worse off than us… but we are quite simply unhappy and unfulfilled. What we really want, is that special someone to come and give us a hug, listen to us and understand, take away all our troubles, complete us and make us feel better. Is it really too much to ask for? And then you look around… and it feels like everybody else has got what you so desperately want.

We become frustrated by the situation we are in because it feels like we have no control over it. We try our hardest but it just isn't happening. It's like we have lost the ability to somehow get our point across, and we aren't even sure how to go about going forward, but the one thing we know is that whatever we are doing isn't achieving the results that we want.

So we stop trying for a while… We try and make do, put on a front because after all, life isn't that bad, is it? But deep down, at an unconscious level, we know only too well that we are kidding ourselves. We are in limbo. We are waiting for better times to come and they just don't. We become resentful, and maybe a bit jealous of those who seem to have it all too. Obviously, we don't like to admit it. It's not that we wish bad things onto happy people, but we're just getting a bit annoyed that our situation isn't right. It can make us a tad bitter but also very sad indeed. It is the sadness that is often difficult to deal with and it can also easily turn to anger.

Acceptance

So once we recognise that there was a problem, we should in essence accept it. The truth is that it is more of an unconscious acknowledgement to start off with, as it is actually quite difficult to really admit. There is an internal battle going on, which is totally normal and a very human reaction.

Acceptance is the most important step but it doesn't come easily, and we will struggle until we reach 'that point'. It hurts to concede that there is something wrong but once we have, we want to 'regain control' and will throw everything at it. Until then, we are just in a state of self-delusion, failing to recognise the reality of what's really happening.

What single people may have tried

There is actually a plethora of things to try. From dating coaches offering to act as your wingman/woman, or teaching you how to use body language in the way of eye contact or flicking of hair, the possibilities are endless! Some even offer to do your online dating profile for you, as well as answer all your messages and see your potential dates before you so you don't waste your time. With all due respect, what could possibly go wrong there? Especially when the number one criticism of online dating is that there is no chemistry? How on earth can a third party help you with that? And what about the actual people looking to date you? Although it actually isn't you they want to date really, because they haven't received a single message from you yet... How would you feel if the shoe was on the other foot and you found out that you'd been chatting to a different person? And how can your own personality come across if someone else is talking on your behalf? Anyway, I just don't get it.

You can also learn dating skills and be taught what the best things to do or say are. Some dating coaches will actually come out with you and show you how to pull. You might be tempted to buy manipulative books such as 'The Rules' or 'How to Get Your Ex Back?'. There is plenty of content online that promises to reveal all the secrets of understanding women, or men, or what you must do to attract either. I have even seen an advert that promised to get you laid without fail and every time (his words not mine) ... Yeah, right.

What people in unhappy relationships may have tried

Again, there is plenty to try here. The obvious one is to work at it - whatever that means to be honest, as nobody has ever been able to really define the term to me when I've asked them what they were doing or what it involved. It seems to be the in word that people generically use. You might have also tried to make conscious efforts or voiced your concerns and attempted to talk, but that's not always very well received. Sometimes, giving it a bit of time so it can sort itself out is also an option. A popular choice is to have some counselling, either on your own or as a couple, or have mediation. There is also a large amount of online resources that you may have looked into. Some people also like to seek general advice to find the reasons why things aren't like what they used to be, looking for answers and explanations in just about anything. Others will throw themselves into work or get a hobby. The unconscious point of this is so that they can occupy themselves; the real issue is then covered, which allows them to avoid the problem altogether. Often, one of the partners will perceive a problem where the other one doesn't at all.

Whether you are single or in a relationship, you will have tried various things to put the situation right. And it hasn't worked so far.

We can't hide from ourselves

Deep feelings and frustrations can sometimes materialise in a physical way, especially when they are left to fester under the surface. These bad emotions often occur when we are not aligned with what is right for us. It is one thing to try and disguise the problem but you will unconsciously know that it's still there. It's the not dealing with the root cause that creates the turmoil.

When we are always waiting and hoping for something to change, it pretty much feels like pushing water uphill. Actually, have you ever tried to push water in an upward direction? I am not trying to be pedantic here and we all know what the outcome would be if we did try. So why are we doing it in our own lives??? We ask ourselves why what we are doing isn't working and we keep on doing it. My old boss always said to me that 'if you do what you've always done, you'll get what you've always got' It's a common saying, in fact it is Einstein's definition of insanity. If we take a simple metaphor like pushing water uphill, we just get it but we don't in our own lives. It's obvious that it doesn't matter how many times you are going to try; it's never going to work unless you change something.

Feeling abandoned

Abandonment may be a bit of a strong word but to me, it actually represents how we feel deep down when we are in that state. You know, that feeling of emptiness, that nobody can help you or understand what you are going through. Basically, the feeling of being unsupported and totally alone, even amongst others. I have faced it a number of times in the past.

If you are in an unhappy relationship, you will have experienced that sensation of feeling as if you were totally on your own, despite having someone sat right next to you. And to be fair, you might as well be on your own because you would probably feel more comfortable. The fact that someone is there with you, but not really with you, will make you feel misunderstood, unsupported and probably not particularly wanted. You will sense the silence even more heavily, as your heart sinks because all you want to do is reach out and make it work. But you appear to have lost the ability to get your point across and just don't seem to be able to communicate properly anymore. You may feel that you would probably get more of a response out of a brick wall.

If you are single and lonely, there is a slight 'despair' to the way you will resent this. It isn't a term I like to use because of its negative connotation (especially in association to dating) but it is the one that expresses it in the best manner. It's the weight of being on your own, and the sinking feeling of not belonging, but longing for someone to be by your side and comfort you.

In both cases, you feel burdened and totally discomforted about your situation, lost and like no one understands you or what you are going through. You're probably not even talking about it to your friends or family anymore as you feel there is little point, going over the same things time and again. Singles begin to dread the question of whether they've met someone yet or how the dates are going, whilst married people will just answer in the most banal way 'You know, the usual…'.

Either way, you are just fed up with the situation.

The danger zone

All of the above will lead to unconscious beliefs about what we perceive to be our problems and frustrations. When we feel pain in that way, our minds will see things in a different light, which will sometimes create unhealthy convictions, about ourselves, or our circumstances.

The best way to explain this is to think of the world around us as 'raw data'. We are constantly filtering information through our senses, so everything that we see, hear, taste, smell or feel. Our brain receives approximately 2 million different bits of information per second, which is why we have that filter. We would be totally overwhelmed without it.

Once everything has been filtered, we create our own meaning. We do this with what we know and can identify; our set of values and beliefs, the languages that we speak, our memories or attitudes, the way we make decisions, our experiences, etc. Remember that all of this is done unconsciously. We then process the filtering through:

- Generalisations – we look for what we are familiar with and expect to happen.
- Deletions – we look for and pay attention to what we are actually interested in, like or expect.
- Distortions – we look for recognisable patterns or connections.

Our perception is *always* subject to these but in stressful times, we will look for negatives and what we perceive to be wrong, so in essence, we are quite literally making it worse for ourselves. We create our very own Catch 22 vicious circle about what we see as the issue, which will feed our frustrations a bit more and reinforce our belief that there is a problem.

We then convince ourselves that we are right, that we know best and that our assumptions are true. We then start to make statements that will re-affirm this to ourselves, such as 'is it me?', 'am I not allowed to be happy when everyone else is?', 'is this my lot then?' or 'there's nothing I can do about it as everything I've tried hasn't worked'.

Our outlook becomes quite dim and pessimistic and we start to get even more down (and sometimes, a bit depressed too), struggling to enjoy some aspects of life. We start to believe that we need to somehow make the best of a bad situation. Our body posture will be representative of that (shoulders might be sloppy for example) and we catch ourselves sighing, sometimes heavily.

Other unhealthy beliefs often are that we need someone else to make us happy and fulfilled or that it is their fault that we are not (and in the case of single people, because we haven't found them yet). You may find yourself saying things like:

- I don't know what to do anymore
- It makes me feel sad
- I guess that's just the way it is
- It's just not happening
- I think I'm getting there, then nothing
- How can I trust that *(fill in the blank)*?
- I've tried everything
- It's just not meant to be, is it?

Unfortunately, these statements will only reinforce what you are already feeling and actually send you further down the downward spiral, every time you have those thoughts.

4

The Reasons Why

On the surface, the outlook appears bleak. You may despair that since as you've tried pretty much everything, it doesn't look like good news, but I am here to tell you that there is good news.

Basically, the reason why you are in the situation you're in at the moment and nothing has worked, is because you have been looking at it the wrong way. This may come as a bit of a shock and will probably surprise you but, in a nutshell, that's what it is.

I touched on it briefly at the beginning of the book and will now explain more. The problems you have been looking at, and feel that you are having, are in reality just the symptoms of the actual real concern.

So literally, think of it as if it was a medical issue. Let's say you have a belly ache and you take a couple of tablets to relieve the pain. It doesn't work so you take a couple more, but nevertheless, it doesn't work. You then go to the chemist's who gives you something else to try but still, the ache doesn't go away. So you end up going to the doctor's, who gives you something else to try. You've guessed it, it doesn't work. At the same time, because this pain is starting to stress you out, you start to develop a headache, so you take a different type of potion. See how you are trying different things but nothing works? And how it can bring on other problems? In the end, the doctor refers you to see a consultant because the obvious solutions aren't working and whatever is wrong with you, is a bigger issue than originally anticipated.

It's the same principle for relationships. You have been dealing with the symptoms of a deeper problem. So what you perceive your troubles to be, are really only the signs of the relationship disease. Incidentally, let's look at the word 'disease'. The Google definition is as follows:

> *'a disorder of structure or function in a human, animal, or plant, especially one that produces specific symptoms or that affects a specific location and is not simply a direct result of physical injury.'*

> *'a particular quality or disposition regarded as adversely affecting a person or group of people.'*

This is exactly what is happening. If you just look at the word again, it can be split in 2: 'dis' and 'ease', in other words, you're not at ease.

Curing one of the symptoms is never going to cure you. If you really want to get better, it needs to be addressed in a holistic way and everything tackled at the same time. I guess it is also a little bit like trying to remove a tree from your garden. You cut the branches and trunk first and after that, you deal with the stump. Once that's done, the next step is to remove the roots. And when they're gone, you then need to remove all the small ramifications that are left behind.

Basically, you have been trying to fix things by putting a plaster on when what you really needed was stitches. And it's not your fault, you just didn't know and didn't realise that you were going about it the wrong way.

Failure was the only outcome
So in your quest to solve the problem, you have looked at each symptom of the disease and addressed them as individual issues.

Because you only ever worked with the symptoms, as opposed to the core issue underlying them all, nothing that you've tried could have possibly worked long term.

If you were single, learning how to flick your hair and make eye contact may have given you a short-term self confidence boost, and you may even have had some dates as a result. Somebody writing your online profile may have made people click on it, and you may have had more messages. You may even have started dating someone. But it pretty much ends there. If what you truly want is a genuine and authentic relationship that lasts, and that is right for you, then you need to tackle the core issue. Otherwise, you will be back to square one at some point in the not so distant future.

If you are experiencing marital problems, going to counselling and talking about the issues may help in the short term. But unless you genuinely feel that you have resolved your differences, feel appreciated and not the one who is always making the effort, it isn't going to fly either. Same thing, the actual deep rooted cause has not been dealt with. If working at a marriage was just about making an effort and talking about the problem, there wouldn't be so many divorces.

What you need to realise is that there is only **one** core issue between you and your ideal relationship. That's what is currently causing all of your problems. Fix it and they will disappear.

It is a process though, and you will need to spend a little bit of time on it, but it will be worth it. It is therefore time for another little exercise, which you can download - **www.sophiepersonne. com/your-other-half-downloads/**.

Perception is projection

I mentioned before about the way the brain processes information and the way we create our own experiences. So, to recognise something, we need to have experienced it ourselves. For instance, as a child, you will more than likely have cut your finger on a knife. Before it happened, you may have been told to be careful but because you hadn't done it yourself, you could not comprehend what it was like. Now, you unconsciously know to watch out. To recognise a problem, it is because it's already within us (to a lesser or greater degree), otherwise we just wouldn't know. So what you will see in others is actually a reflection of you. Everything that you feel, see or hear from the outside, is processed by your brain and then represented internally. The moment you consciously form a projection or a judgement about anything, a person or an idea, it becomes your perception.

This is how you have identified with some of the symptoms and some of the solutions that you've tried.

We live in a world where it's extremely easy to compare our lives with other people's, as we are so connected. There are plenty of resources and platforms available for us to do so. Take Facebook, it is probably the number 1 place where we form judgements on a regular basis. Actually, pretty much each post that we read. We form opinions all the time, which is totally normal.

In prehistoric times for instance, where we had little interaction with others, there wasn't that many of us around and you'd only come across approximately 50 other people in your lifetime. Therefore, we would have had a lot less chances to do so and we wouldn't have compared ourselves to others to the extreme that we do now. In those days, it was about survival and for most of the Western world at the moment, it's about 'quality of life'. 100 years ago, we still didn't have access to that many people. Of an evening, you would have either been on your own or just with a handful of other individuals. We started to have more opportunities to compare our life with other people's when televisions and mass consumerism started. But we are now bombarded with opportunities to feel inadequate and judgemental, and often from the comfort of our own home. And a lot of us unconsciously will feel that our lives could be better. It gives us a warped sense of expectation and normality.

Let's look at what 'normal' is though. A quick Google search returns the following definitions:

'conforming to a standard'

'the usual, typical, or expected state or condition'

But what is usual or typical? This is all well and good if we are talking about body temperature for instance, but in a more human and psychological sense, there really is no such thing as normal. What I consider normal will most probably be totally different to what you see it as, and this is where we again perceive and project. We start to make generalisations (which I have touched on before). It is the basis of our learning so what we have experienced before, or what we have witnessed in other people's lives and that we can recognise and associate with, becomes our expectation of what a normal life should be.

It is worth reminding ourselves on a regular basis that people lie and aren't always honest with you, or themselves for that matter.

We all know this, but will forget from time to time (especially when all we see in our own life is doom and gloom). The way they portray themselves and their relationships makes us feel terrible. We all have that one happily married friend that just rubs our nose in it all the time or the one who is really popular and has the best life in the world...

Remember that you don't know what goes on behind closed doors. It is commonly said but it's true. So many people put this façade up because it makes them feel better about themselves. It's not real though and couldn't be further from the truth. It makes them feel good to know others are watching their 'perfect life' from the side lines. However, it then becomes what you unconsciously see as the norm and aspire to.

It's the same in all aspects of life to be honest, just look how parents will compare their kids and what they do; from the age they started to walk or talk to the wonderful university course they have just started, or their amazing careers. We know how people exaggerate at times, but because it's about something that we care about, we are more susceptible to feel that it's the norm. We basically always seek reassurance that we are doing the right thing and we are more likely to believe something to be true when we perceive some form of social proof: if these people are doing it and if they believe in it so much, then it must be right. It's the bandwagon effect that will influence us.

So through this, you can now start to realise that actually, what you are seeing as 'normal' and your expectations, is based on something that isn't necessarily real or a lie.

That's not all though

Because of the way we absorb information and create our own reality, truth and lies are only perceptions anyway.

Another one of the NLP presuppositions that I want to talk about is that 'the map is not the territory'. What this means in simple terms is that what we see isn't the whole picture, but just what we chose to unconsciously focus on, and is based on our experiences and expectations. I recently witnessed an argument which was based on a misunderstanding. Misinterpretations and confusion are often how conflicts start. For simplicity, we will give the two parties names, so Mary and John. At a party, Mary misheard something that John had said, which upset her. John realised she wasn't looking particularly happy so asked her what was wrong. She was sulking and only half answering him but he worked out what the issue was, so explained what he had actually said and put things straight. Mary appeared to understand she had misheard what he'd said so it was left at that. Some days later, John happened to mention the episode and was surprised to realise Mary was still upset by it. He reminded her that they'd had a conversation about it and had explained what was actually said. He was then bewildered to hear what she said next…

'Oh, I didn't realise that, I didn't hear you
say that because I was so upset.'

Mary was so focused on the fact she was sad and troubled that what John told her didn't even reach her brain. Her attention wasn't on any of the words, she had expected to be let down so the information was distorted.

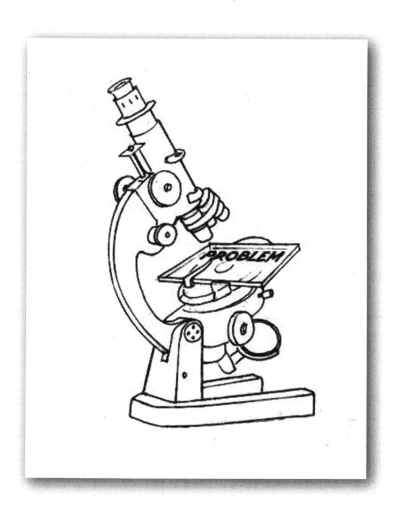

This is how we create our own reality. In this example, Mary was actually miserable for days because she felt hurt. She had obviously been disappointed in that way before and her brain processed what had happened as it believed the outcome would be. Her view of the world was misrepresented.

We actually pay more attention to what we see as evidence supporting our beliefs and experience. We will even ignore evidence that doesn't. If something has happened to us in the past, we will see signs even when they're not really there. We also like to think that we can control outcomes, especially when we have recognised what we see as signs. Our brain fools us, purely because it has happened to us before. In the same way, if we like one particular trait in someone, we will probably like the rest. This is actually known as the halo effect.

So now you understand that the reason why nothing has worked so far, is because you have been fixing the symptoms but not the core issue. It is purely because it's often misunderstood, but now that you are on your journey and starting to understand where it went wrong, we can start to tackle the actual deep root cause in the next chapter.

5

The Real Problem

So we now understand what the symptoms look like and how they represent themselves, we also recognise the way some of our beliefs don't serve us. We can comprehend the reasons why what we may have tried in the past has failed and we are ready to identify what is actually stopping us to live the happy and fulfilling life we desire so much.

It's a fairly uncomfortable concept to start off with, but is really key to the pursuit of the journey.

Common wisdom makes us believe many things. In heterosexual relationships for instance, rumour has it that the reason why dating and relationships are so difficult is because men and women are different. Apparently, we want different things and we need to change our personality, our character to adjust to each other. There seems to be a belief that we are poles apart and all I want to say is:

FALSE.

First of all, I will agree that men and women are wired differently and have very specific traits. I won't however go into that too much here, as there are enough books and materials on the topic. What these fail to tell us is that ultimately, we probably all want the same thing, and it is to be happy. End of. Whichever way we choose to go about it, and what represents our perception of happiness is neither here nor there, it is our one and only goal.

Secondly, I also disagree on the fact we should change for somebody else. There is loads of advice out there specifically designed just for men or just for women, how we should act in front of the other sex, and how to make them do this or that. I personally believe it's a lot of rubbish. We should never change our core selves for someone. What needs to happen, in any relationship, is to learn how to understand the other person better, as an individual and not because of their gender. We can adjust the way we communicate with them to make sure our message gets through but not manipulate them. That is just not right. Healthy communication is the basis of everything and creates a better experience for everyone.

It is crucial to recognise that the only person you should wish to change for is yourself. And when I say change, it needs to be taken with a pinch of salt. What you have gone through the years will have made you a certain way. It isn't about making you someone you're not, this is about understanding how some of your life experiences have shaped you and why these actually make you react the way you do. It's about discovering who you really are and your purpose, realising what behaviours serve you and which aren't so helpful. Are there patterns in your existence? Things that keep on coming back? History repeating itself? It's about identifying the difficult situations from the past. You'll know the ones I mean… They are those that you have put in a box somewhere at the back of your mind, 'never to be opened again'. Only sometimes, the box lifts its own lid and some of the stuff inside leaks out. You try to jump on it as quickly as you can to close it again but it has just reminded you of its presence.

All of these things consciously, but more importantly unconsciously, taunt you. They are at the root of all the self-fulfilling prophecies and self-limiting beliefs that you keep on re-affirming to yourself. You don't even notice that you're doing it because you're so used to it. The vicious circle keeps on going. And on growing.

Unfortunately, I see many people who are misguided and think they are in control. They usually dismiss any suggestions that there could be more than meets the eye, as they believe they don't need to look at themselves. After all, they have the answer already, haven't they? They are also the folks who normally don't have the best of relationships. The truth is, that's because they don't really understand themselves nor the deep root cause of their struggles.

And here is why.

The relationships that we have are a direct reflection of the relationship we have with ourselves.

There you have it. The key to successful relationships is that you need to have a good one with yourself first.

So the people that I have just described above fall into one category, which we will call 'The Ostrich'. They will argue that they know all about it, that they practice self-love and they will be adamant that 'they are number one', … blah blah blah. The Ostrich will unfortunately do what we know an ostrich to do. It is actually a myth but as the saying goes, it will put its head in the sand because it doesn't want to acknowledge the problem or deal with it. To be fair, it isn't the fault of The Ostrich, it's just not ready. And that's absolutely fine because ultimately, we are all responsible for the choices we make and our own happiness. I don't however, want to have to hear The Ostrich moan about its problems ever again, because the decision has been made to do nothing and hide. Therefore, there is no surprise it is still experiencing the same issues and actually, now deserves them.

If the people who say they know themselves and already do everything they need to do but are still struggling in their relationships, then to be frank, they are quite clearly not applying their own set of principles.

But one day, when they are ready, and when they lift their head outside of the sand whilst nobody's looking, they will.

The relationships that we have are a direct reflection of the relationship we have with ourselves.

So it's about us. We are the one person who can fix the core issue and the way to successful relationships is for you to become a better version of yourself. It's about being at peace with the past and the difficult situations you've had to deal with. It's forgiving yourself for what you regret, or wish you had done differently and keep on beating yourself up about. It's about being true to you, be honest and comfortable with the truth, happy inside. Once you achieve that, you will have very little stress in your life.

Taking responsibility

As we discussed in the previous chapter, we create our own reality. It is important to understand that in exactly the same way, we create our own happiness. Nobody can do that for us, they really can't. We do and we are responsible for our own happiness. We often look to others to complete us. One of the metaphors often used in relationships is that people fit like two jigsaw puzzle pieces, but the truth is that you complete yourself. Other people only add to your life, you complete yourself through your own choices and taking responsibility. If you're not happy single and in your own company, you won't be happy taken either. Yes, we all want companionship, we seek someone to share experiences with, but to make it the best relationship you've ever had, you need to accept that the buck stops with you.

Letting go of the outcome

This is especially true in today's world, where we are made to be driven by goals, outcomes or deadlines. We put enormous pressure on ourselves to achieve what is often set for us.

By accepting yourself, you start to accept others for who they are too as opposed to the person you'd like them to be. We are made to believe that we can control situations but we never do. We think that we do and we try really hard, but what you need to do is to somehow let go. To tell you the truth, it's easier said than done! But it's key. We cannot control people or situations; we can only control ourselves. Interestingly, I have an example of this, which has literally just happened. A close friend of mine's partner has just left him. I won't go into the reasons but what I will say is what he has just told me.

> *'I didn't say how I felt by fear she would leave me. I thought that if I tried to control the situation, it would be ok and yet, the outcome is still the same. I should have been myself regardless.'*

In the same way that we simply cannot (and mustn't) change for somebody else, we equally can't make someone make us happy and we can't control our relationships. We all have free will; we just need to choose what we do with it carefully.

So now that you are starting to understand the concept a little bit more, you can see how it changes everything. It is the only way you will solve your problems. It isn't your fault, you just didn't understand that it was the real deeper core issue, and this is why what you've tried before didn't, and couldn't, work.

The truth is that once you know and accept your wobbly bits in terms of emotion and pain, you will learn to let go and become the true you. Once you have become the better version of who you are, as opposed to changing to attract a date, or trying to get your own way and make someone do what you want in a relationship, everything will fall into place. If we go back to the 'perception is projection' concept we explored earlier, and that what we recognise outside of ourselves, is actually to a lesser or greater degree already within us, you now understand that what you see in somebody else is something that you can see in yourself. Your own reflection.

There is a simple exercise that can be done to explain this further. Think of someone you don't like very much, and think of the reason why they rub you up the wrong way. Now look at yourself and be honest. You either have the behaviour that they display, or you had it at some point in your life and you just don't like to look at it, because to you, it's not something good. I actually did this with 2 people I knew and didn't like… I was actually quite horrified (for want of a better word) by what I found out about myself, but I decided to face it. I identified that at some point in my life, I had displayed those traits and I acknowledged why it made me feel uncomfortable. Incidentally, the two individuals in question are now friends of mine.

In order to make all of this even more relevant to you, please go and download the two work sheets I created (**www.sophiepersonne. com/your-other-half-downloads/**).

So the issue comes from me?

In essence, yes it does. It's not easy to accept but the quicker you take responsibility, the better. As we can't change people, it is actually the best way possible. Isn't it? Once you recognise that it comes from you and as you start to understand why, it will become quite simple to fix. Until you do, and without realising it, you also need to know that you are sending conflictual unconscious messages.

So if we take the example of a single person. The problem isn't that he or she doesn't know how to flick their hair or that they are a bit shy, it actually goes back to the relationship they have with themselves and the unconscious message they are sending out to others. Let's say they are lacking in self-confidence. Tricks on how to use your body language in dating situations will give them a short term boost, but it doesn't remove the deeper issue. Why are they shy? Is it because they have been rejected in the past? Is it because they had a bad experience as children? Was there a time when they were ridiculed? Are they just a quiet person who doesn't like the attention to be on them? All of these possible explanations call for very different ways of approaching the problem, and until they do, they will struggle. If you were unwell, you'd go and get it sorted so why not do it for your own happiness? I sometimes hear things like 'Oh but if I had someone, it would sort itself out...' To be blunt, that's totally delusional and the typical response of The Ostrich.

What we all need to concentrate on is this: where is the problem actually coming from?

It is important to understand how we create our experiences. A lot of our learning comes from a one-off event or through repetition. For instance, you study the alphabet by repeating it time and time again, but other things are learnt by the reaction that we have. When you were little, you were probably told not to touch a knife as you would get cut, or not to touch a flame as you would get burnt. It is an absolute guarantee that you will do it at least once, but because it hurt when you did, your brain learnt to never do that again. It works in the same way for everything. Unfortunately, I can't go through the entire process here, as I would do with my one to one clients, because it is something that is tailored to each person, but you can start it yourself. So if you are the shy person we were talking about earlier, you need to establish where that lack of self-confidence has come from or you won't get results.

In many examples I could give you, it basically boils down to:

- Facing your demons
- Finding and releasing the inner deep root cause
- Understanding your trigger points
- Learning to care for yourself

Once you do that, everything will start to fall into place. There is actually little point in looking to someone to save you because it really isn't going to happen. And yes, I know it does in Hollywood movies and fairy tales, which is why we dream that it would, but they're not real. The truth is, only you can save yourself. Nobody can make you happy or complete you, it's a state of mind that you will only achieve yourself.

Experience has a structure and we have a strategy for everything that we do, from brushing our teeth to opening a door or lacing our shoes. We unconsciously do all these tasks and we do them in the order that we learnt. The way you put the toothpaste on, run the water, hold your brush, all of this is done through unconscious images, sounds and feelings that are familiar to you. This why people can perform on auto-pilot because there is no conscious effort to most of our daily activities. Consciousness will only occur if there is a disruption in the order we do the task. For instance, you are tying your laces and all of the sudden, one breaks. Your conscious mind will automatically kick back in, as the brain is now confused and has to quickly deal with the fact that it quite literally, hasn't gone as planned.

So before you can sort any type of relationship issue, you need to understand why and how you are causing the issues.

You need to consciously fathom your strategies, address the problems and accept that the outcome that will follow, is right for you.

Your Other Half

So just to reiterate the point...

The relationships we have are a direct reflection of the relationships we have with ourselves.

I think that the easiest way to describe this concept is for you to think of yourself as a mirror; basically, what you see is what you get.

In English, the term 'other half' is often used to describe a partner. There are some variations of it but this is the most commonly used. It isn't actually what I want to focus on here. We all have 'an other half' within. We could easily represent it as a large suitcase, which is filled with all the things that we have gone through and see as bad or painful. There is also an added section where we store our flaws, and all the little things we don't really like to think about too much because they make us feel uncomfortable.

We all have a darker side, no matter how good a person we are. It is just one of those theories that there must always be two sides like yin and yang, or light and dark. Think of the moon for instance. The far side, which is often referred to as the dark side, is only visible some 18% of the time. This is due to tidal locking with the earth and is why we only see one side most of the time but it illustrates the point perfectly. This dualism is in us too and we all have a dark part. It is rarely seen or consciously visited as we don't like to explore it too much or too often, because it has a habit of triggering unpleasant emotions or making us cringe.

'Everyone carries a shadow, and the less it is embodied in the individual's conscious life, the blacker and denser it is.' – Carl Jung

Over our lifetime, we have saved all our difficult memories in there. It hurts to go there and remember them. Some of us might also find it tricky to acknowledge the suitcase but it's always there, hidden away.

Another NLP presupposition is that 'mind and body are one system'. Strong reactions (good or bad) are normally very vivid and the brain can't differentiate physical danger from emotional danger. When we experience something painful, it quite literally goes into shock. Because it hurts so much, it will do its best to protect us and help us survive. If we were to actually feel the true intensity of the pain, it could actually kill us. Heartache has very genuine physical effects: the brain feels the same way whether you are physically or emotionally hurt. It will match the pain with the experience that it remembers and our hormones sky rocket, affecting the same part as addiction and cocaine craving. The adrenaline levels go up and we go into fight or flight mode. It has actually been known for people to suffer sudden heart attacks (and subsequent death) when they have had to face intense emotions. This is also why anxiety attacks will often manifest around the solar plexus area as chest pains. In some cases, the pain will even radiate to the jaw or the arms. With the heart pounding so hard, it feels like you are being punched from the front and the back at the same time.

Fear and uneasiness can also make us feel frozen and struggling to move our limbs. We are literally numb, which is how our brain wraps us in cotton wool to shield us.

These painful events represent our dark side and are stored away in a place that we don't particularly enjoy visiting nor necessarily like to share openly with the world. This gloomy dwelling in our head is where we keep all of the emotional baggage and all of the little things that have affected us in life, from our first difficult interactions as a child to the more obvious break ups we will have had in our love life. In there, we also hide what we see as flaws and what could be improved upon, the bits of our character that we don't like so much. All the bits you try to cover up when you start seeing someone and that will come out through time. All of these also unconsciously contribute to our representation of our own self-worth.

The best way to describe Your Other Half is that it is the elephant in the room. You very much know it's there, but you will skirt around it and pretend it isn't. Addressing the problem feels unnecessary and the risk of going back there far outweighs the benefits.

The thing is, unless you re-explore what hurts, you are going to struggle to get to the other side as it were. When we don't deal with things, they pretty much come back to haunt us. They creep up in the middle of the night, when you can't sleep, and just decide they are just going to sit on your mind. They make you feel uneasy or sad. They sometimes appear in your dreams too. Every single thing that you do not address, you will carry unconsciously. This can also trigger uncomfortable feelings, which can't be interpreted as they should and leave you feeling rather anxious or on edge.

The aim however, is to embrace Your Other Half, warts and all, because it is what makes you, YOU.

It is very common to hear people say that 'you have to love yourself for who you are before people can love you'. I personally feel it isn't so much about loving yourself but accepting yourself. Acceptance of Your Other Half, the dark side that you conceal, is what will allow you to have better relationships because you don't have anything to hide anymore. The stress is gone. Even if you think that you aren't hiding anything, unless you have done the work, you are and it will prevent you from moving forward.

This is potentially a lengthy example but relevant. One of my coaching clients was struggling to decide whether he should leave his marriage or not. He had been unhappy for years and the relationship was certainly not going in the right direction. He wasn't staying in the marriage for his wife, but purely for the bit of paper that represented the promise he had made in front of all his friends and family years ago. The real reason why he couldn't leave however, was in his past. He'd had a child in a previous relationship but after the birth, things went very wrong between him and his partner. He made the hardest decision of his life and chose to leave. The guilt of having failed at the relationship, and leaving his daughter behind, were the real reasons why he was frozen into indecisiveness. Despite numerous attempts at saving the marriage, he was too scared of what it would say about him as a person if he did go. The problem was that he was extremely unhappy. Unconsciously, he knew what he needed to do. Instead, he was creating more guilt and actually doing a disservice to just about everyone; his wife obviously, but also his child. His daughter could pick up on the unconscious message he was sending out, and on his emotions. This was making her a bit reluctant to spend as much time with him as she would otherwise have done. But more importantly, he wasn't being honest with himself.

Incidentally, creating better relationships doesn't mean forcing things to work. Sometimes, it's about having the courage to face your elephant, and realise that whilst things could have been improved if they had been dealt with before, you are now too far down the garden path. It is sometimes better for both parties to split up, allowing each other to actually find happiness.

One of the things that stops us from addressing these issues is a fear of the future and what it might bring. The apprehension that, if we make the wrong decision, things are going to be really bad. Actually, it's a trick of the mind. There is absolutely no way for you to fear the future because it doesn't exist yet. It hasn't been made up, so there is nothing to worry about. It's about your mindset and what you project onto your perception of the future. Let me explain this with the example of a 2-year-old little boy and his favourite teddy bear. The teddy brings the child feelings of love, comfort and security, it makes him smile and feel happy. Now, think of a time when the bear is forgotten somewhere or lost. The angst of not having the teddy brings sadness, tears, screams, insecurity and anxiety. All of these feelings are 100% coming from the child, the teddy has no input whatsoever in how it's making him feel. Recognise the situation and the symptoms? Now translate that to your fear of the future. It isn't projecting back onto us, is it? It is quite simply a trick of the mind that, at times, we can all be guilty of.

We should all trust in ourselves and our ability to make the right decisions or deal with difficult situations in the correct way. Imagine that you are in your car, driving during the night to a destination you don't know. You might have a sat nav or a map, but that doesn't tell you what the road is like or where any potential obstacles are going to be. The next curb is in the future, and because you've never been there, you don't know (excuse the pun) what's around the corner. Your lights are on but they only light so much of the road in front of you, yet you trust that you will get to your destination without any major hurdles. You don't even ask yourself about it, you just trust that you'll get there. And eventually, you do. So why is it so difficult to trust yourself to make the right decision?

Incidentally, the married guy I mentioned before, did eventually make up his mind. He left. His biggest regret? Not looking into himself before so he could understand what was stopping him. He can't believe he wasted that much time and didn't do it sooner. His now ex-wife is happy and with someone else. His relationship with his daughter has improved dramatically because the unconscious message he is now giving, is one of inner peace and happiness.

Our unconscious message to others

We don't always realise it, but we unconsciously pass our emotions onto people. I have already covered the NLP presupposition that states that we cannot not communicate but this is slightly different.

We may think that we are particularly good at hiding some of our feelings and we may believe that nobody will see through our poker face, but we're not. When we are out of alignment, people know. Not necessarily consciously, but they'll get the vibe. If we take the chap I've just mentioned as an example again. In his mind, he was covering his unhappiness well, the façade he was putting in front of his family and friends was water tight. His daughter knew instinctively, and without ever being told, that there was a problem. She could pick up on the atmosphere for a start, but she could also unconsciously recognise that her dad wasn't as happy as he had previously been, and that he was that little bit grumpier about things in general for instance. It is even more obvious today, as their relationship has blossomed since he left the marriage. He can still be grumpy obviously but in a different way. That's because he is now happy and relieved as opposed to frustrated and anxious. In the case of his wife, she knew all along that things weren't right. Some of the arguments would have given her a clue but it was the unsaid that she picked up. She could feel his unhappiness, which in turn would make her unhappy too, and on the defensive. In tense situations where no outcome is reached for a long time, the relief experienced when it eventually does is greater than we would anticipate. We may not always want a particular outcome, but at least we are out of the limbo state. Deep down, we know what's right in the long term and for the best.

I have come across a number of clients who struggle to be honest. What I mean by that, is that they find it extremely difficult to tell others how they really feel for fear of upsetting them. As a result, the communication often breaks down, as it becomes an exchange of unconscious messages and vibes that don't go hand in hand with how the person is acting.

Gut instinct

They say that the gut is the second brain and this is very true indeed. We all have a gut instinct, and we should always listen to it but we often don't. We listen to the voices in our head more, telling us how fat we are, that we aren't good enough, that we should do this, that or the other... or we listen to our paranoid and absurd inner talk about all the things that could possibly go wrong in our lives, but very few of us actually properly pay attention to their gut instinct.

In my particular case, I have certainly learnt in the last few years, that decisions made with the heart are always right and the ones made with the head aren't.

Our head will always look to what is rational and what we 'should' do. We base our decisions on the basis of what other people think, what is seen to be right or wrong in society, and what we ought to want. Unfortunately, what is perceived to be right for us isn't and couldn't be further from the truth. Going with what you feel, and being aligned with your true self, is the right and only way to go. We always know if we should or shouldn't do something, especially when we go against it.

A friend of mine had to make a decision once about a new relationship, which had the potential to be 'the one'. He actually chose to leave the lady, in order to be able to follow a different career path. He believed it was the right and most sensible thing to do. He had extremely strong feelings for her but in his head, wasn't ready and prepared to take the gamble. He justified the decision to himself, and others, with a million of well-rehearsed and logical reasons. Inside, he was totally destroyed. After telling her what he felt he needed to do, he was actually physically sick and threw up. His gut was telling him it was the wrong thing to do because all of his emotions were negative and he was feeling horrible. He regretted his decision for months and never really got over it.

We all know deep down, if what we are doing is what we need to do and right for us. If we feel angst, stress, anxiety or any of these bad feelings, then it's probably the wrong decision. I recall a time when I took a particular job because on paper, it would be silly not to and (little voices starting in my head) I really ought to, and it was more money, and more responsibilities, blah blah blah, … It wasn't actually what I wanted to do but I went ahead anyway. The last time I didn't listen to my gut instinct was 5 years ago, and the consequences were such that this time, I've learnt my lesson. It was to do with a relationship, which I knew I needed to walk away from. But I didn't. I had more than enough opportunities to do it but still, I didn't. The worst thing is that I knew from the very start it was a bad idea. The outcome was a lot of stress and aggravation, losing a lot of money as well as having to get an injunction against the individual. Now, I only make decisions based on how I feel, and

I can positively say that it is serving me just right. Don't get me wrong, there have been times where I have actually questioned my own sanity because I've really been going against all the rational good reasons my head has given me. It didn't always work out as I thought, but it worked out because it was the right thing to do. At the end of the day, if something makes you feel dread, anxiety or sadness, it's not the right thing to do. If it makes you feel hopeful, joyous, excited and full of anticipation, then go for it.

Sometimes though, and especially at the beginning of trying to listen to your gut, it's not always easy to know which way to go or even what it is telling you. After all, what's the difference between being suspicious and having the answer? It's quite straightforward. Mistrust is when the little voices are talking to you, and having the answer is the way you feel. The easiest thing to do if you're still unsure is a very simple game of 'heads or tails'. Ask the question, determine your yes and your no, flip the coin and whatever side it lands on, you will know from your reaction. You will either feel 'Happy Days' or a bit of a sinking feeling in your stomach. You then know what you should be doing.

Reaching the acceptance stage

So now that you are starting to understand the importance of accepting yourself, I just want to reiterate that once you have, you will be more aligned with your beliefs and values than you are at the moment. You need to understand your own deeper issues, and how they have moulded you into the person you are today, before being able to move on and have the relationship that you truly want.

We have mentioned before that one of the NLP presuppositions is that the 'map is not the territory', but it's important to be reminded that we all have different maps of the world. Yes, it's obvious and you know that, but the odd prompt doesn't do any harm. We can all be guilty at times to believe that we know best, and to try to change the opinions of others. It is completely normal because our beliefs are based on our experience, and after all, we may want to help people avoid the mistakes that we've made for instance, or just put our point across. The problem comes when we think that our views are 'better'. Yours is not the only truth. Imagine I was sat next to you right now. You close this book and we both have a look at the cover. We wouldn't see the same picture because we would look at it from our own reality and angle, you would pick up certain things that I would miss and vice versa. We have already discussed how we create our own reality through deletions, distortions and generalisations. Both our maps of the world are true and very real, but different. When people start to think that others look at things exactly like them, they end up confused. And when they start to believe that people should look at things in the same way that they do, they end up disappointed.

We often can't understand why someone behaves in a certain way or why they do certain things. We will shake our heads in despair, judgement or bewilderment, but we forget that from their map, their actions make total sense. We are judging them from our map, which is why it's incomprehensible. What we need to do is to get to their map and then look at the world as they do, through their eyes. Once we do, we can better understand their position, instead of believing that they are wrong and we are right. Incidentally, that's just arrogance because we are all right and wrong at the same time. Our truths are different. Arguments are only arguments because we are stuck in our own world and retreated in our own trenches. An example of that is actually one of the complaints I hear regularly from one-to-one clients when they start to work with me. Things like 'It's not right!' or 'You can't do that!', are the typical way of responding when we judge and want others to be like us. We are right and they're wrong. We are hurt that they can't see this, so we say it even more and try our hardest to make them accept our point of view as their own. When they don't, we then proceed to read them the riot act and unsurprisingly, it falls on deaf ears. Hardly a surprise is it? Once you start to look at some of the differences of opinions you've had in the past, think how you could have handled them differently if you had tried to see them from the other person's perspective. Would the outcome have been different?

Expectations and assumptions

So with everything I have just explained, you can now see how you have only been trying to solve the symptoms of a deeper rooted 'disease', which is to be at ease with Your Other Half. One of the common signs is that you start to expect things from others. Statements such as 'I deserve to be treated properly', 'I deserve better than being treated like that', or even 'I'm fed up of having to make the effort all the time' highlight that we anticipate a date or partner to act in a certain way, without any input from our side. So whether you are single or in a couple, the problem is that you expect a significant other to make life better for you, and that's quite simply not going to happen. I will be blunt here but you actually are the one with the problem, and you need to sort it yourself. If you don't drop your expectations about others, you will always end up disappointed. The only person you should be expecting anything from is yourself. Whatever you get from others is just a nice surprise that you should be grateful for.

A few years ago, I was on a training course, and it was presented to me that the word 'assume' was clearly defined as such: 'making an ass of you and me'. The definition of an assumption is pretty much the same as the one of expectation, which is:

'a strong belief that something will happen or be the case, without proof'

Assumptions and expectations go hand in hand. But based on the fact we create our own reality through the way our brain processes and filters information, what exactly are we founding these on? It is a fairly straightforward answer; basically what we want and wish for, which is fine. We are all allowed to have desires and dreams. But then, if we analyse the process of an expectation, it becomes a bit ridiculous. Basically, we actually want someone else to be or do what we want and wish for, without telling them that's the case, but anticipating them to guess and do it. In the case of single people, we create an image of the person that we would like to be with, and then end up disappointed because 'they're not like what they said they were' or their pictures. Yes, most probably... but it's not their fault, is it? We saw what we wanted to see. We **hoped** that they would be what we wanted, but when we find out that they are not, it's their fault and they've let us down. Is it really? Can you see that everything was your own perception of what should be and that you then projected it onto others? Expectations will only lead to disappointment. That is just the way it goes, but most of us do it. We feel that people should act in a certain way if they really liked us.

There is absolutely no point in looking to others to make us feel good or provide us with whatever we feel we deserve. The truth is that we are responsible for our own happiness and shouldn't seek approval or look to someone to make us better, in exactly the same way that other people are responsible for their own lives and creating their own bliss.

However, expectations are common as it is another unconscious behaviour. They are also not often voiced. We expect someone to do something but we don't tell them, and then assume they know. And we wonder why we end up disappointed!? By doing so, we create a warped idea of who the other person is, instead of looking at who they truly are, and accepting them as that. Expectations make us try to change people, as we unconsciously want to mould them to what we believe is right. The fact is that people will only change through their own life experiences and what they encounter, not because we want them to. Their main traits don't normally change and if they do, it's only temporary. In reality, these will probably accentuate as they get older.

I can actually think of hundreds of examples where we believed someone would do something but didn't, and then had the audacity to claim they knew nothing about it. I think assumptions and miscommunication are a bit like the chicken and the egg... Not sure which one comes first. The end result is rarely positive though. We are not in this world to live up to other people's expectations so why do we want them to live up to ours?

Using a different approach

So you can now see how we are our own key to our own door and how, with just a little bit of knowledge and understanding, you come to realise that you need to fix the relationship you have with yourself, before you can fix the ones you have with others.

You have made an effort and worked at things, but you haven't had a result because these 'things' weren't what needed to be addressed.

Your own emotions and Your Other Half are what needs to be dealt with first, as well as what you are currently unconsciously feeding through. You are otherwise disguising yourself and the problem further. If you still believe that what is stopping you from achieving your goal of either meeting the right person for you or sorting your relationship/ marriage, is other people, then I'm afraid to say you are wrong and delusional.

Fix the relationship with yourself, before it's too late and before life has passed you by, then the rest will follow. You will only get results by using a different approach than that you have used in the past.

6

The Choice Is Now Yours

So now that you understand where you have been going wrong in trying to sort out the symptoms as opposed to the deep root cause, it is time for you to make a conscious choice about what you are going to do next. Before you do though, let me tell you more about the concept of expansion and contraction. In a nutshell, everything either grows or shrinks, there is no middle ground. If you look at a plant, it will either grow or die. If you look at metal, it will either expand or contract depending on the temperature. Nothing can sit still, it is physically impossible... Therefore, this concept also applies to us and our feelings. Even if you are totally feeling in limbo, as if nothing is happening in your life or stuck in a rut, at some point, something will happen. It's a bit like the wheel of fortune, it goes down but it can't stay down because of the momentum. At some point, the wheel will go back up, it's just the way it works.

You actually have the power to take control, not of the outcome, but of yourself and your happiness. When you start the journey, you will not know or see the destination, nor how long it will take you.

There are 2 types of people...

Some of you will already be ready, and some of you won't be just yet but it's only a matter of time.

I have touched on this a little in the last chapter but let's call the first type of person, the one who isn't ready, The Ostrich. The Ostrich is uncomfortable with the truth and will hide from it, will find excuses and reasons as to why it shouldn't look within. It will do what an ostrich is known for and quite literally bury its head in the sand. It's easier that way, to blame the world for everything that's not working how we want it to. The Ostrich is a bit fatalistic and will not take responsibility for its own life or happiness, it's everyone else's fault.

On the other hand, we have The Tiger. The Tiger has recognised he needs to sort things himself, he has accepted the challenge, is proud of what he has achieved so far and wants to take control of himself. He will fight and hunt for the prey, do what's required, taking both responsibility and action in order to get what he wants. The Tiger will reap the rewards.

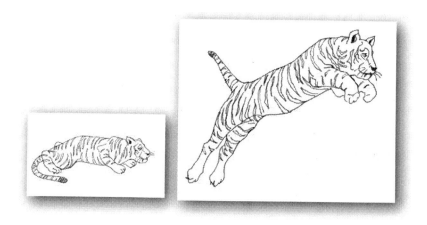

In the same way we looked at expansion and contraction, it is obvious that The Ostrich will shrink and The Tiger will grow.

It might sound harsh, and nobody really wants to be The Ostrich. Deep down, we all want to be The Tiger. There are times in life though, when we are The Ostrich. It's just easier to hide behind excuses, because we are genuinely scared. Sometimes, it isn't even the fear of confrontation, or to face up to our own demons, but actually the fear of happiness. And that's when we hear all the little voices in our heads again, telling us all the self-limiting beliefs and self-fulfilling prophecies we are used to hearing on a regular basis.

So you might start thinking:

- I don't believe in it…
- It's a waste of time…
- It's a gimmick anyway…
- I don't need to change, I'm not the one with the problem…
- That's just stating the obvious and it won't make a difference…
- I still think it'll sort itself out in time…

Change is uncomfortable, and we often feel a bit confused or scared before it takes place. Things may have happened to you in the past, but now you have a chance going forward. The more you try and fix other people, or your marriage, or your dates, the more you are going to feel the problems you are currently having. What was, and still is, presented to you as a solution by society isn't looking at the bigger picture and therefore, completely superficial. This is why it hasn't worked before, isn't working now and won't work in the future. As I've said previously, Einstein's definition of insanity is to believe that you will get different results by doing what you've always done. If you repeat the same actions over and over again, how can you get a different outcome? Do I need to say anymore?

The deep rooted issue is that the relationships that we have are a direct reflection of the relationship we have with ourselves. They are the people we choose and attract.

Let me share another NLP presupposition with you:

People have all the resources they need to succeed. There are no unresourceful people, only unresourceful states they get into.

For clarity, a state is your mood. So a resourceful state would be if you were feeling happy, motivated, raring to go, excited, etc., where an unresourceful state would be if you were grumpy, angry, frustrated, cynical, dismissive, etc....

We often let what is around us affect our disposition and the way we feel. For example, let's say you didn't sleep particularly well last night, and just as you managed to drift back to sleep, the alarm went off. You then dropped your breakfast on the floor, had to rush because of having to clear up the mess, got in the car, and you are now following the dumbest of people driving at 5 miles an hour. As if you weren't annoyed enough, every single set of traffic lights is either red or turning to red as you approach them, so you are now late. What's your mood going to be like then? Probably not the best... And how difficult is it going to be to turn it around and make you feel happy? I'd say that at this point, you have probably unconsciously already written the day off. It's an easy thing to do, because we are all human and sometimes unaware of our reactions. By the way, this isn't about pretending to be overly happy when you're not feeling it. This is about recognising the signs.

The power of the mind

Through life, we all experience good and bad. Unfortunately, because of our very own and very efficient self-criticism mechanism, we normally wallow in the bad more than we do in the good. If someone pays us a compliment, we first have to accept it, which a number of us struggle to do. Let's say that we take it gracefully, we will then feel good about it for a while, but the minute someone tells us something that we don't like, we will seethe about it and probably remember it for months to come. It's also worth remembering that we are used to being 'put in a box' from an early age, as we are told not to touch this or that, because it burns or cuts. At school, we are told not to talk because the teacher is speaking. At work, HR, Health & Safety, your boss, budgets or anything you can think of really, will also regulate what we can and cannot do. So we end up in a world full of negatives where we don't really allow ourselves to believe we can get what we want. It's the same in dating for instance; once we have been on a few dates that have not turned out to be what we wanted, we kind of expect more of the same. We come to unconsciously believe the worst is going to happen.

I am not sure if you have ever heard about the Law of Attraction but it's a fairly simple concept. Like attracts like. So the grumpier you are, the more red traffic lights you are going to come across basically. You attract what you focus on and think about. Think of a magnet; the negative cannot attract the positive. This is why people who keep on talking about how ill and unwell they are for instance attract more of the same. I know a particular person who is obsessed by water leaks/ floods. She's always talking about it (not the most thrilling subject of conversation either), and I have to say, I don't know anybody who has experienced more of them than her... 11 in 3 years to be precise.

If we focus on what we do not want, that's what we will attract. The more negative we are about something or a situation, the worse it normally becomes. A simple shift in your mindset could totally change the outcome. It's not always easy, and we sometimes need a bit of help in recognising that we do it and catch ourselves. There are a few simple things that you can do to start initiating a different result. It's all in the mind. Set it to what you want, as opposed to what you don't want. As Henry Ford said:

> *'If you think you can do a thing or think you can't do a thing, either way you are right.'*

Believing that there is nothing you can do about your situation, or that everything is out of your remit, will bring what you consider to be failure and no results. Beware of being overly negative, as this normally leads to frustrations and a whole new vicious circle. So the idea is for you to change your state and in order for you to get to your desired state, you will need to use your own resources.

Every behaviour has a positive intention

This is another NLP presupposition, which can sometimes be difficult to believe but it really does. As explained previously when we touched on strategies, our unconscious mind is in charge for the majority of the time. Most of what we do is learnt, so you don't need to think about the step by step process when you make tea, brush your teeth or open a door. You are on autopilot. It is your conscious mind that looks to the future and rationalises what you should or shouldn't do. Your unconscious makes you act in the moment, so when you let it make decisions, it often resorts to what it knows best to start off with. In most cases, that would be the parental programming we received, our experiences, peer pressure or society. It doesn't work with logic or words but with feelings, most of which you will have learnt either through repetition or one-time events (which are often traumatic). I know we have covered this before but it is worth bearing in mind for what I am just about to say.

So your unconscious mind is on your side, whatever it does. It can be difficult to comprehend that there is a positive intention behind everything but there really is. One of the best examples I could give you is this: you have just come home from work and it's been a long day. You get in and deal with everything that needs to be sorted. Once it's all done, it's time to sit down and relax. You kind of want to have a treat... In my case, it would be a glass of wine, but you might prefer to have some chocolate or whatever your guilty pleasure is. And here commences the battle, which we will represent with two characters. So, on the one side, you have a little devil sat on your shoulder and he is telling you that you deserve it, because you've had such a hard day. You've worked hard, it will make you feel better and (he then reiterates), you just deserve it. On the other side, you have a little angel and he is telling you that you really ought not to, because it's not really good for you. Think of the calories, you've been so good this week so far. Think of your organs, it's not really beneficial for them either, is it? So you are now having these two, arguing out what decision you should make. They both actually have your best interests at heart. Obviously, the angel is thinking of your health, but the little devil is also looking out for you, because he wants you to reward yourself for having achieved so much today, and make you feel good. So even when we do things that are detrimental to ourselves, there is a positive intention behind our actions. Now think of a time when what you may have done upset someone else, or how they might have hurt you. It wasn't necessarily intended that way and there would have been a constructive purpose.

So if we take this back to The Ostrich and The Tiger, both have positive intentions behind the way they act and react. The Ostrich wants to protect you from pain and upheaval, where The Tiger wants you to be happy and move forward.

The purpose of negative emotions

A negative emotion is designed to draw your attention to a problem so you can do something about it. A good example to relate this concept to, would be when you are driving your car and the fuel light comes on. What it is saying to you, is that unless you put some juice in it, the car will stop and come to a halt in approximately 50 miles. Straightforward. You now have the choice to get to the petrol station and fuel up, or run out and walk. Either way, a decision is made. In this particular case, it's a very easy one to make because I can't think of many people who would select the option of effectively, breaking down. In terms of Your Other Half though, you quite happily carry it around through life and when it manifests itself, telling you it needs sorting, you ignore it.

Let's have another motoring scenario. So you've been to the station and your car is now full. You are on your merry way somewhere and, all of the sudden, the oil light comes on. At the earliest opportunity, you check the oil, and put a bit more in. A couple of weeks later, the oil light comes on again but you remember that it actually wasn't that long ago that you had a look and topped it up. You check it again just in case and the level is ok, so all good. However, this keeps on happening randomly so after a while, you don't really bother checking it anymore because you know it's a quirk of the car. It's going in the garage soon anyway so you'll get them to have a look then. Basically, you've got used to it. And it is pretty much the same in your life right now, it's a familiar feeling. Wouldn't you prefer to be able to have no warning lights coming on and interfering? Because the reason why you are in the situation you're in, is purely because you have become used to it. How will you know if there is a genuine problem with the oil pressure before you go to the garage?

Negative emotions control some of our responses. Have you ever witnessed someone reacting way too much to something? Are there some people that just push your buttons? The truth is, sometimes, you're not really reacting to them but to a situation that happened long ago and that is engrained at the back of your mind. Once you have dealt with Your Other Half, your negative emotions will not need to keep on showing up, because there will be no reason for the warning light to come on. That is all they are, a warning system that lets you know something needs to be addressed and motivate you to do something about it.

Unfortunately, when these negative emotions are left unresolved, they tend to attract more of the same. Remember that the unconscious mind doesn't deal with logic or words but feelings. When something hurts us emotionally that badly and with such vividness, your brain will remember it. As soon as something remotely similar happens (or we perceive it to), the brain will react in the way it knows best. You create adverse momentum and feed it.

So now, you are ready to be The Tiger!

Even if you don't feel ready right this minute, you will be very soon, because you now understand why you were The Ostrich at some point and how much of a disservice it has been to you. What we resist the most is what we need the most.

We cannot be in control of the outcomes but we can be in control of our lives and happiness. We do this purely with our own will to make it happen. Think how exhilarating it would be to start the journey and:

- Accept responsibility for the results you are getting
- Look within to who you are
- Discover your own strengths and weaknesses
- Deal with your troubles
- Stop being held back
- Improve yourself and your conditions
- Accept others and their opinions
- Curb expectations and assumptions
- Trust in yourself and your higher self to get it right
- Believe that your relationships with others will improve once you have fixed yourself

It is worth bearing in mind that nobody is asking you to change into something that you're not. All you need to do is to face up to Your Other Half. You will then create new ways of responding and interacting, as you get a better experience. Remember that the reason why it didn't work before, in what you've tried, is because the root cause wasn't dealt with. It wasn't your fault; you just didn't know.

How life will be different

This isn't about getting what you want from others all the time, this is about having a harmonious time and experience with them. It is about removing petty conflicts and wasting time on individuals that do not serve you. Once you know yourself properly, you will begin to understand other people too, and how they see their own corner of the world. Because of that, you will be able to relate to them and get their point of view, even if you disagree with it. For couples, this will cause less arguments. It will increase the love and affection that you have, as well as the way you show each other, simply because you both have a better daily life experience. For singles, it will allow you to attract people aligned to you as opposed to Your Other Half, give you the tools to recognise the signs and pick wisely, or walk away, in your own power. You will be more confident in your choices as well as assertive. You will stop waiting around 'just in case', you will have assurance and take action.

The reason why it will work, is because it is the answer you have been looking for, as opposed to popular old fashioned advice that only looks at certain aspects of the problem and states the obvious. You know, the stuff that you have read about or heard 10,000 times before. It isn't about common sense, it is about a deeper meaning which is the ultimate benefit. Once the work is done, you will have a new found happiness. It will allow you to love and respect YOU, truly, relying purely on yourself for fulfilment, and only looking to others to add to your life as opposed to being a crutch, or carrying you and your emotions.

As we said, when you've lived with a problem for a long time, you get used to it, so you don't notice it so much. When the problem is no longer there, you realise the long list of ailments it used to cause you.

This is something that my coaching clients often comment on. They just can't believe that they were carrying such a weight. As it literally lifts off their shoulders, the sense of relief can be overwhelming.

Just imagine what it would feel like to stop pretending everything is ok all the time, to be less anxious about the future, stop being in limbo and waiting for something to happen. Wouldn't you rather enjoy life and the process? Once you are happy inside and in your own relationship with you, you will start to allow a flow with others because the unconscious messages will be true and positive.

7

The Solution

A ccepting that the relationship that you have with other people comes from you is the first step. Becoming The Tiger, and getting your head out of the sand, are actually probably the hardest things that you will do because they represent your commitment to taking responsibility for your own happiness. After that, it's actually quite easy. The way you tackle it will be very personal to you. There is no right or wrong approach and you will pick the one that suits you the best. Some people like to work on themselves on their own. Others prefer to seek professional advice as it makes the process quicker and smoother. The guidance and support through the journey is important to many but if you decide to go down that route, make sure you choose the right person to help you.

Whichever way you choose to do it, you must remember that what matters, is that you are doing it. I would like to share some simple steps with you that will get you started on your journey.

Be yourself

One of the most common complaints in the early stages, is that the partners change and aren't the same person that they were at the start. This is actually one of the main reasons why relationships fail in the first few months, and one that could be easily avoided. Obviously, when we first meet someone, we emphasise our good points because we just want to make a good first impression. This is a completely natural and unconscious human behaviour, but often causes problems when we revert back to type. We also sometimes consciously change some of our personality, because we worry that if we show a particular side (Your Other Half), it will be a deal breaker. The truth is, there is only one way to have a successful relationship and it is to be honest about who you are from the start. In my case, when I was younger, I wanted to show how strong I was, and how I could handle everything without showing any signs of weakness. As a result, I attracted quite a few people who were very needy. I was the rock they wanted and I was carrying them through life. But I wasn't as strong a rock as I liked to portray. I'm actually quite an emotional and soft person underneath it all, so it didn't serve me at all. I resented them in the end because they weren't bringing me the support that I needed. Needless to say that these relationships did not last. We often forget that life is a journey, and as we go through it, experiencing the good and the bad, we change and we grow. It is worth taking some time out every now and again to remind ourselves of who we really are and what matters to us. Only once you know yourself and are truly honest from the start will you be successful in dating, growing as a couple and staying strong.

Of course, being on your best behaviour the first few times is totally normal and what you should do. The problem comes when you start accepting or doing things that don't resonate quite right with your own values and beliefs, or your interests. We are not all going to be the same, and whilst we should have some similarities, it would be very boring if we didn't have some things that differ from our partners. It's when it just doesn't feel right... Again, it's actually all about gut feelings. Do you feel like you are dreading a particular outdoor activity? Or the fact that you will just be watching movies and not go out all weekend? At the beginning, we don't always care what we do, as long as we are spending time with that special person. But it is worth doing your own self checks... If the person didn't want you to do this, would you? Regularly?

This is why it is so essential to know who you are and what you want. If you are for instance a home buddy who doesn't really enjoy the outdoors or live music, there is absolutely no point in starting a relationship with someone who wants to go out and enjoy either of those activities every single weekend, however well you get on. It quite simply will not work long term. You will start to resent going to these things and will probably unconsciously try to change the other person as well. It seems obvious but you'd be amazed how many people make that mistake. So knowing who you are is the first step. Acknowledging and recognising the signs that there is little point in trying to become someone you're not, is the second.

'We must not allow other people's limited perceptions to define us.'- Virginia Satir

When you are part of a couple, you have obviously already gone through this bit. The foundations are set but now that you have been together a while, you might find it difficult to be yourself. Life pressures, having to compromise... It is important that you take the time to explore who you have become. What influence has your partner got on you? Is it healthy? It's about nurture. We are constantly reassessing our relationships, without realising it. We can feel when they change, but only unconsciously. The power shifts from one side to the other depending on what's happening around you. Outside events or peer pressure can affect the dynamics and as a result, make either party change ever so slightly. You need to be able to question all of this to learn who you have become and allow your partner to do the same. Both of you will then need to rediscover each other.

In any relationship, we seek common ground. We seek those 'like us', in our values, beliefs, hobbies, likes or dislikes. This is why we struggle when people change. Remember that nobody will ever be totally like you though. It's the little differences or quirkiness that help to make the relationship last and what it is, more interesting and exciting.

Being yourself is good for the soul. All too often, we pretend to be something that we're not and it is actually quite stressful to keep it up. There is little point wearing different masks with different people. We do it for fear of not being liked where accepting ourselves and our flaws is actually much more satisfying. It brings an element of peace because it means we are surrounded by the right people. Honesty is an essential part of any relationships and it starts with us.

Are we seeing what we want to see?

It can't be stressed enough that getting to know someone properly is very important. I want to add here that it's obviously essential when we first meet them, but just as vital to keep learning about the other person through the relationship. If things are turning sour, it's something you need to do as soon as possible.

All too often, when we find someone that we really like and start seeing them, we just rush into things without taking the time to really find out about them. It is unintentional, we actually think that we need to know as much as we can, and spend as much time with them as we can too. With all the excitement and promise of what could be, we don't always pay enough attention to what they are actually saying or doing. Instead, we see what we want to see or we hear what we want to hear. As I have explained before, when we like a trait in someone, we are more likely to find other qualities that agree with us and our map of the world. This is why our brain is working overtime to just see those bits.

We focus on what we want to see, because we want to be reassured. We want to see the positives and we want to think that they are perfect for us. Attention to detail is essential; actually, you need to quickly establish what the other person's 'flaws' are, so focusing on the negatives will serve you in that instance. You need to know what they are because some you can live with, and some you can't. We are all different and certain things will matter to us where others don't. Remember that we all have our own little quirks too... Sometimes, something that seems like a minor detail and of little importance, will actually demonstrate that you both have very different values. This is where it is worth mentioning again, the importance of knowing yourself truly, as well as your own ethics, beliefs and life goals. If they differ from the person you are with, you are probably setting yourself up for failure.

Taking the time to really get to know someone is, in essence, the foundation of whether the relationship will be successful or not. Obviously, it is a lifelong process anyway, as we will all change and evolve with age, but the core normally remains the same. A lot of people don't always understand why you have to invest a lot of time and emotion into finding out how compatible you both are. There is simply no other way. It is not an easy task and it can leave you feeling like your relationships never work, or don't last any more than a few months. This is normally the point where we can become open to settling with anyone, just because we want to feel loved. To be honest, that's the worst thing that can happen but it does. A lot. It's where we normally go into desperation mode and close our eyes to what we don't want to see or don't like, because we don't want to be on our own. This can also create the foundation for future upset and separation.

Again, there is also a lot to be said about listening to your gut instinct. We see those things that we are really not so sure about but we don't do anything about it. I know that I certainly tried to silence the internal red buzzer a number of times over the years and that never served me... Quite the opposite and that's how I ended up having to get an injunction out on an ex-partner. So if you feel there's something that you just can't put your finger on, take the time to discover what that is. Keep in mind that you need to dig further when you are unsure about something; don't ignore the signs.

Always remember that honesty at an early stage is paramount. There is absolutely no point in trying to overly impress the other person because at some point or another, the real you will emerge. This is the point where relationships fail because 'he/she has changed'. Someone should love you for who you are... Yes, it's a common statement, but just because you really like someone doesn't mean that they are right for you, so always be yourself, or it simply won't work. Once you are part of an established couple, honesty is just as important. Say it, whatever it is. It's better than festering in your own corner and bottling things up.

So is it ok to tell her that her bum looks big in that? Yes, absolutely! But it's how you say it. If you just say 'yes, your bum looks big in that', you will probably have something thrown at you but if you reply in a constructive manner, that shows that you care and pay attention, then she will be very grateful. The way to do it is quite easy. All you have to say is something along the lines of 'this cut isn't so right for you but your blue/ red/ pink/ black (fill in the blank) one is and makes you look really good', or words to that effect.

Say what you mean

We often think we know how to communicate well, especially with those we are close to. After all, they know us, so they should know what we are saying? They don't, I'm sure you now understand that. You must always say exactly what you mean, to the point and without hinting. It isn't always easy because even when we are aware that's what we should do, we don't always take the time to think about our message. Sometimes, we don't really realise that how we say what we say might affect someone. We can also apprehend difficult conversations and delay them. Unfortunately, this only means one thing; usually, when it does come out, it normally isn't in the most helpful manner. Never avoid talking about what you feel may be a challenging topic, just make sure you prepare for it and how you want to come across. Being unclear in your communication will actually lead back to the vicious circle of expectations and assumptions. People will probably read too much/ not enough in what you have said too.

It is also important to talk about the 'little things' in your life. This is especially true in long term relationships or with people you don't see very often. It becomes very easy to become strangers, as you will no longer know the other person if the minor details aren't shared. The little nothings often become the big things. It is common to find that in struggling marriages, you may know the person and their habits (i.e. how they like their tea), but you haven't got a clue about who they have become and grown to over the years. One of my coaching clients had been married for 35 years, yet going through the process with me, she realised that she didn't know her husband anymore, and nor did he. But she realised that and did something about it. In her case, it wasn't too late, and I'm pleased to report that they have gone from strength to strength.

When you talk to somebody, make sure there is rapport between you. It doesn't just happen, it's a process, and the easiest way to do it is to align yourself with the other person. It creates trust and harmony and is essential to get your point across.

Make time for yourself, but for others too

Time is probably our most precious resource, so making time for anyone will always make them feel special and good about themselves. Isn't it nice when someone actually does that? It makes you feel wanted and cared for. Whether it's family members, friends or a romantic relationship, it's important to spend some genuine quality time together in order to create memories and keep things alive. In couples for instance, it is especially important to share moments such as meal times together. It may be a bit difficult at times but it's essential to avoid becoming flatmates and just sharing a house. If you don't make time for each other, you start to drift apart. In the corporate world, companies organise team bonding days to make sure staff spend quality time together. This is exactly the same principle, it is done to help create and sustain good working relationships, make them grow and has real value.

When you make time for someone, you need to ensure it's enjoyable. Couples in long term relationships or marriages are often guilty of not doing this. Routine, kids, work, just life in general can get in the way, and both individuals end up leading separate lives. Going on holiday together is one thing, but it's mainly about enjoying each other's company on a daily basis. Not doing so often leads to trouble.

Pay attention

How many of us just don't do that? We have a chat whilst replying to a message on our phone, whilst the TV's on, whilst we check on something in the kitchen. Ensure that you properly listen to what is said but especially to what isn't said. Communication is 7% words, 38% tone and 55% body language, as previously mentioned. Paying attention to non-verbal clues will make you more approachable, and you'll understand more of what is really being expressed. Then you actually get what the other person is really telling you or how they are feeling. It really does help to spot potential issues before they happen.

Paying attention to someone is also about making their problems your own. This isn't about finding solutions but just being there for them. Sometimes, all we want to do is just to talk and vent. When you are facing a difficult concern, knowing that there's someone there to support you and that you are cared for makes all the difference. Ensure you have kind gestures for the other person. Again, this isn't just true when you are in a relationship. Bringing flowers to a friend for no reason, or your boss giving you a bottle of wine just because, all of these little attentions are nice. More importantly, they will make you do more for them because you feel valued.

Looking to your past

I'm not going to lie; this bit isn't particularly pleasant but it's crucial. What you are looking for, are the main themes in your life, which you will have established from the exercises in the previous chapters (go to **www.sophiepersonne.com/your-other-half-downloads/**), and how you can get them back to their original point. There is normally a thread that leads back to a one-off event or repetitive similar occurrences that will have created a particular problem. This often leads to a traumatic situation and it isn't always an obvious one. Ask yourself what your first memory of the experience was and work from there. This is where you have to point the finger at yourself as opposed to everybody else. It will hurt before it gets better but once you've got to the bottom of it, this stuff doesn't ever need to be dragged up again because you will be ok with it.

You have to ask yourself some fairly difficult questions, and instead of looking at what others may have done to you, you need to assess what you could have done differently and the part you played, because we all do. We just don't see the signs at the time. As the saying goes, there's often two sides to a story, and then there's the truth. We create our own reality remember and we often see what we want to see.

If you are single and attracting a particular kind of person, you need to dig deep. The answer lies where you haven't dealt with the emotional baggage properly at the time of the split, or moved on too quickly. One of the main reasons why singletons come to see me is usually because they feel trapped in a vicious circle where they only attract the same kind of potential partners. The description of these can fall into many categories but the ones I actually hear about the most are 'players', 'weirdos' and 'princesses'. So if that's the case for you too and you really can't work out why, here it is... The primary reason is you are not aligned with what you want and this goes again from not having dealt with Your Other Half properly. Most people who have been single for a while are likely to have the same observations as to why they are still on their own. It's rarely their fault, it's just that they haven't met anyone, or the people they do meet aren't good enough or a certain type, or it just never lasts.

There are often many reasons why someone will be single and struggling to attract the right kind of person or hold a relationship for more than a few weeks. These are often very personal to the individual and sit deep in the unconscious mind. Unfortunately, this is the seed of why we then either appeal to a certain type of person or just cannot meet anyone. It hides in the unconscious mind, it creates the way we behave and what we do. There will be certain patterns of behaviour in common and will share some of the mistakes they make. Another reason why people may struggle with dating is simply that they aren't happy with who they are as a single person. This is absolutely key, as the signals that they give out will determine the responses they will get. It's the unconscious messages that I mentioned before. This is where some singletons are often seen as being desperate. In their communication, they imply that they are looking for someone to save them in some way, and this will come across very strongly. As I've said, we should look for someone to enhance our life, not to fill a void that we can't or don't want to fill ourselves. This is actually very unattractive for most. So it is crucial to learn how to enjoy our own company and do what makes us happy, **before** starting to look for a partner.

Another cause is that despite everything, they actually aren't really open to opportunities or even recognise them. We are often too quick to judge on looks and just entertain what we see as eye candy. It's actually a pet hate of mine; we all age, looks fade. The long list of demands on online profiles is just as ridiculous. After all, tell people what you have to offer instead of creating yet more expectations. Talking to people for who they are and just enjoying their company is what we should do. After all, the average person knows approximately 300 people. If we get on with them, it's because we have something in common, so it is likely that we will also like their friends and get on with them. They have friends too... So be open-minded because it opens up to a huge network of opportunities. Let's not forget that feelings often grow from getting to know somebody. So if dating is a bit of a struggle, maybe the simplest way to sort it out is to look at it differently and just look to enjoy life... The rest will follow.

If you are in a relationship that isn't working but you always have short relationships, the answer is also in finding where you went wrong in terms of a major split. By major, I don't mean necessarily in terms of how long you were with the person, but the intensity of feelings and the way it ended. If you are in a long term relationship or are married, you are looking for 3 different types of issues. First, it could be something obvious that changed the dynamics with your spouse (cheating, feeling badly let down, routine has just killed the couple, ...). Second, look to your past. If we take the example of the married man that hadn't dealt with the guilt of leaving his daughter behind, that's the kind of thing you are looking for. And last but not least, a combination of both. Once you have determined what your deep root cause is, you need to add to it. If we think of the elephant in the room, it started as a fairly thin creature and now it's massive with meat to its bones, so what else has contributed to it? And how is it triggered? Is there something you can do to take its lead and move it out of the room? An example of that could be to talk to someone from the past about what happened and seek answers, or even apologise.

When a relationship ends, people often forget to allow themselves to take some time to grieve. It doesn't matter how long you were together, it is an essential part of moving on. Those who leave the relationship have often already gone through that part, whilst they were deciding whether to leave or stay. The ones who didn't choose to end it are frequently left to wonder what went wrong, but rarely take the right steps in assessing the situation. They often move on very quickly and leave themselves open to unhealthy patterns forming.

Learning from the past

The first thing to do is to ditch blame. Putting all the wrongs on the other one will achieve very little. There is rarely only one person responsible for a break up, as our own behaviour will influence how others react to us, so reflect on yourself as a partner too. There is never just one side to a story and whilst we may not like to see it, we would have played a part in the failure of the relationship so once again, accepting responsibility is a massive step forward.

It is also essential to look at why it didn't work out and what, if anything, could have been done (and at what stage) to change the outcome. As the saying goes, 'hindsight is a wonderful thing' and yet, we don't often take the opportunity to look back when we should. What other way have we got to learn the lessons?

And it is about the lessons. Your lessons. Everything you need to identify and deal with if you want to really move on. Once you have worked out why the relationship ended, it is important to look at the person you were with. Assess their good and bad points. What qualities did you like about them that you would want to find in somebody else? Analyse what you enjoyed and what worked well in the partnership, as opposed to what didn't so much. Concentrate on the positive aspects, not what you don't want and like. If you are in a relationship now, does your partner have these qualities? Do you mind that they don't (or do)? What is working well for the both of you and what could you improve? Try and establish whether you are the only person to have the problem, or if they do too. Recognise what the solution is, and who should instigate it; you, them, both?

Also, be brutally honest with yourself. Should you have got together in the first place? Sometimes, we just go along the rollercoaster of emotions, just because it's nice to be wanted and have a bit of company. But was/ is it all really working as you wanted it to? All too often, we just let ourselves slip into a routine and accept things that we wouldn't normally, because we don't want to rock the boat or be alone. Hollywood movies suggest we should find the right person straight away, which couldn't be further from the truth. We are all on a journey of self-discovery, which can only happen as we meet new people and let them enter our lives. There are no failed relationships, just lessons we have to learn in order to grow. Then we can be sure of who we are, comfortable and happy in our own skin, not looking to somebody to make us complete. It is at that point that we are ready to find and accept the right partner for us.

Analysing the real reasons behind a separation is key. This is just as valid if you are currently having marital problems, get in there quick and before it's too late. Let's be realistic, we don't go from really happy to really dissatisfied overnight. Sometimes, people have been unhappy for weeks, months or even years, so it's important to establish what really happened, look at the signs that we could have picked up on and how both parties handled themselves. We normally can see there is a problem, but we become The Ostrich. It is the accumulation of all the small things that creates the bigger issues, but once we have identified what the root cause of the problem was, it is unlikely we'll fall in the same traps.

Do you know what you want?

This is one of the reasons why it is so important you deal with your emotional baggage and discover who you are. Once you have, the next step is to know what you want. We think we do but most of us don't. With everything you have learnt so far, you can now assess if what you believe you want, is from your own doing or if it has been influenced by others (parents, friends, society, etc.).

When we are single for a while, we end up falling in one or more of the following categories. You either just can't meet anyone, you attract the wrong types, the people that you meet aren't what you thought they were, the chemistry isn't there or it just doesn't last. Nowadays, the easiest way to meet a new partner, regardless of age, is online dating, so most of us will resort to it at some point. (For the record, I hate online dating but I won't go on my soap box about it now). You normally start off being quite rigid and selective in terms of your search criteria, but there is often a time where you'll start to entertain people you normally wouldn't. Whatever means used to meet people, we are all guilty of sometimes ending up just going on dates that are a waste of time or indeed dating people that are just plain wrong for us, 'just because you never know'. Hopefully, with what you have learnt so far, that will no longer be the case.

So when I ask people if they know what they want, they always say yes. Then most of them will start reeling off a list of all their essentials and no-no's, what the person should look like, what job they should have, blah blah blah, ...I call this 'the checklist' and I can't stand it. Not only is it very superficial, it's not what it's about. In a nutshell, this tick list is normally where they go wrong. It rarely reflects the person's deeper needs and is one of the reasons why relationships don't last. Granted, chemistry is vital. But we forget that chemistry doesn't just come from looks. It is something that happens whenever we come into contact with a new person, be it a neighbour, colleague, someone in a shop, etc. Chemistry also comes from getting to know somebody, their intellect and the emotional connection that both people will form together. Relationships that last are normally based on those foundations. Actually, ask anyone who has been in a couple for a long time, they will know that **and** tell you that. So why is it that when they become single again, they forget that bit...

So yes, chemistry is essential. But what about the rest? As I've just said, most people think they know what they want but they don't really. It is essential to know who we really are, what makes us tick, what our values are and what we stand for. Take a bit of time asking yourself these questions because we change as we grow. What we want evolves over time and is affected by our relationships. Is what you want what you really want or have you adopted that belief because it was put onto you? I certainly know that when I did this exercise on myself, there were things I thought I liked but actually didn't. It was just that I went along with it years ago but it doesn't serve me. When we are with somebody, we will also develop some of our tastes together, which is a very good thing if both are genuine.

This is why discovering who we are and what we want is so essential. Only once we have done that, can we start to form an idea of how to proceed in relationships. The secret is to know yourself. You may actually surprise yourself once you understand fully how events from the past have really affected you.

It is empowering to take charge and to change the course of your life for the better, so once you know what you want, you can go and get it. Once you do, you can start to notice what happens, and what follows on from that. It is however essential to remember to respect other people's maps of the world. You now understand how it works, but remember that they don't necessarily. You have more tools than them and it is down to you to lead the way. I recall a particular client who didn't have the best relationship with her mother. She had very strong beliefs about her and why she was acting the way she did. We used a technique called Perceptual Positions where in essence, you put yourself in the other person's shoes. She was quite amazed to realise that she was wrong, and that her mother was reacting to her own childhood.

She had created her own defence mechanisms and was actually screaming for help. The lady was therefore able to use the tools she had learnt to help her mum. She could lead conversations much better because she understood where the issues had come from, as opposed to guessing and assuming. Get in rapport with the other person.

I also need to remind you that we can't control outcomes. Another NLP presupposition is that 'there is no failure, only feedback'. In a world of goals, pressure and deadlines, it is difficult to bear that in mind. After all, if you don't succeed, it can only mean one thing right? You failed. I'm here to tell you that actually no, you didn't. The way you tried needs tweaking or changing, that's all it means. The response you got only indicated that you need to try a different avenue. We think we know how things should turn out, but we don't, we really don't. Very few people didn't imagine their life to turn out the way it did, but it has. That's why it is feedback as opposed to failure, it is a mechanism meant to guide you in the right direction.

'Winners, leaders, masters – people with personal power – all understand that if you try something and do not get the outcomes you want, it's simply feedback. You use that information to make finer distinctions about what you need to produce the results you desire' – Tony Robbins, Ultimate Power

Reframe your thoughts

This is another NLP technique which will help you to see what happened in a different light. It should also be used for future events, and throughout life, as it will assist you to understand people and situations better.

Basically, we cannot change the events of the past and the content of your experience will always be the same. But you can change the context and by doing so, you also change the meaning. Remember that we create our own reality through our senses and the way we process information. Wherever you are right now, look around you. If you change seats, your environment will still be the same but you will have a different angle, and what you'll see will be totally different.

It is the way we frame the events in our life, or the actions of others, that determines their meaning and therefore our feelings. Reframing them, and establishing the positive intention behind someone else's behaviour, will give you a better insight. Remember that people like to be treated as they treat others. This is purely because the way **they** are and what's acceptable to them. For instance, when I travel back to see my parents in France, the very first thing my mum will say to me, is that I should sit down because I must be tired. Basically, that's what she likes to do when she arrives somewhere after a long journey. However, I am totally the opposite. I prefer to sort things out straight away, go and refuel the car, do some shopping. Then I can relax. However, I understand her behaviour so instead of getting annoyed with her because she keeps on telling me to rest, I just say to her that I will in a minute. We all know that we see things differently but we don't always understand what it truly means. This is why expressing opinions and different points of view can easily turn into conflict.

Another NLP presupposition, which I wanted to tie in with what I have just said, is that the 'meaning' of communication is the response you get. People will respond to what you give them. Most of us will have had an argument at least once. If you feel someone is aggressive and attacking you, you are very likely to respond in the same way. Until one of the parties starts to back down, the situation will escalate. If you choose to be the person who decreases the intensity of aggression, you will be able to pace and lead the other person. If you smile at someone, it's likely they will smile back. This actually reminds me of a particular experiment I did a few years ago. I was really grumpy at the time and I mean, really grumpy. I can't remember why or what had triggered it but in any case, it called for emergency wine. I decided to walk to the shop to try and calm down. So off I trot, face like thunder... It was actually a nice day and there were quite a few people about. I decided to try and snap out of it by smiling to the people I'd come across. The first one I smiled to clearly thought I was deranged. Because I had to force the smile, it probably just looked like an open mouth with lots of teeth sticking out. I'll never forget the look he gave me lol... I carried on though, and the smiling became more natural and less scary. By the time I got to the shop, people were smiling at me first, purely because I had managed to change the mood. So remember that you can control the result you get back. For instance, you are unlikely to carry on shouting at someone if they look apologetic and actually saying sorry.

You will recall what we spoke about when I mentioned strategies, and how we all have a step by step process for daily activities. In the same way that you can reframe your thoughts, you can change the structure of a strategy (as you can't change the content). For example, the finger of God. We normally see it as if it was pointing at us and possibly a little threatening, as if we've done wrong. Who is to say this is how it should be seen? What if I told you the finger isn't pointing at you but just about to caress the top of your head? We get stuck and too wrapped up in what we want to see, remember. Loosen up and shift your position. The outlook will be very different.

The Discovery Frame

You won't consciously remember when you were born but you will have probably been in contact, at some point in your life, with babies. As they start to develop and grow, and in any new experience that they learn, their level of consciousness is pretty much zero. This is because they have not had the experience yet, so their brain doesn't know how it's going to respond until it happens. In NLP, it's called the clean state: you haven't learnt from outside influences yet. The first time you crawled, or had sweets or sprouts, you didn't know how you were going to react. Each new learning programmes your brain. It is how you have become who you are today, as it imprinted good and bad responses in your mind.

The discovery frame is basically about going back to being a baby. You consciously pretend you have no experiences, you drop all of your expectations, assumptions and judgements. You also let go of your attachment to a particular outcome. Once you have done that, look at the situation with new eyes. What does it look like? What's the outcome? It does take some practice when you're doing it on your own but once you have mastered this technique, you will feel a lot less stressed and much more at peace. This is because you are not expecting, or craving for something to happen, so you won't be disappointed by an event, a situation or even someone. Instead, you will have opened yourself up to new possibilities but especially to learning and growth. Let go of trying to control situations and allow new and unexpected opportunities to enter your life. When you stop fighting, it simply happens. You don't have to think about it or worry, you just allow different experiences to come your way.

Alignment of self

This is a concept fairly well known in self-development circles, but not everybody will be familiar with what it means. One of the Google definitions is this:

a position of agreement or alliance

For most people, it simply translates to being happy. It's when you are in that place where you feel joy, harmony and at peace. You are on purpose, you feel connected to your life and the people around you. The fears, the anxiety, the frustrations, they're all gone; it's bliss. It's the feeling that you get when you follow your gut instinct, the sense of anticipation and happiness that you experience. Your higher self actually wants you to be aligned all the time because it means you are happy and connected. The problem occurs when there is a disconnection between our conscious and our unconscious. This is why The Ostrich will be completely out of alignment, because it knows it but isn't accepting it.

In order to tackle each symptom one by one, I like to use a NLP technique called Logical Levels. It allows us to find where a problem sits and where to make the changes. This method has actually been criticised by some, but I have had so many results for my customers from it that I use it regularly. From top to bottom, they are:

- Spirituality/ Purpose
- Identity
- Values & Beliefs

- Capabilities
- Behaviour
- Environment

The way to use this is to take the particular problem you are experiencing and ask yourself questions at each level, starting from the bottom. It is worth noting that the higher levels have more leverage. Let's take the example of self-confidence. Is the environment at play? For instance, someone might be quite assured at work but shy in a social environment. Moving on to behaviour, what is this person doing when they are in that state? It might be that they are wringing their hands, have sweaty palms or go very quiet. Then looking at capabilities, this person knows that they can be confident. Basically, you would keep going until you find the right level.

I will just share a bit about my story here. I mentioned earlier about the nervous breakdown. Once I'd accepted that it had happened, I knew I needed to get to the bottom of it. I actually believed that I had managed to sort out my Other Half but quite clearly, I hadn't. I will cut a very long story short. In my case, the root causes were rejection and pressure. Don't get me wrong, we all get rejected, and we all have a problem with it. I won't go into details but because as a child, I was very sensitive, nervous, very naïve and trusting, with a soft nature, it affected me in a very significant way. This rejection wasn't just about the obvious either, I have plenty of examples. This is actually why I put on such a hard shell. I just didn't let anyone in, not really. As you can imagine, it affected all my relationships. The pressure element came from being a perfectionist and the way I was brought up. Through fear of disappointing, I had never actually allowed myself to be myself.

I won't bore you with the details but I did a lot of work. It did take time, mainly because I was doing it on my own. However, I can now say I haven't got any major stresses in my life anymore. I am totally aligned with who I am, what I do, my dreams and I am connected to my source. Don't get me wrong, I'm still human and I still get wound up by little things but the weight I was carrying is gone.

I have applied the same methods on my clients and it has worked for all of the ones who really wanted it to happen. This is why I know that if you do all of the work in this book, truthfully and whole-heartedly, you will reach alignment. It may not be through the outcomes that you expect, but it will happen, purely because you no longer have anything to hide. The weight of the world will fall off of your shoulders and you will feel lifted.

8

So Now You Know...

So you now understand why the relationship you have with others is a direct reflection of the relationship you have with yourself.

This chapter is really to summarise what you have learnt. Some of the concepts I have introduced to you in this book may be new to you, so it may be wise to go back through them.

It is important to remember that life is a journey, so don't kick yourself for not being where you want to be just yet. You now have the tools to take control of your destiny. As humans, we feel impatient and we want things to be as we want them to be, right now. Just remember that we are still in essence animals. We have certainly evolved in some ways, and actually so has the way we have relationships.

If we go back to the cavemen times, the relation between a man and a woman was mainly about survival. The dating scene at the time was as far from thrilling as it got because as I mentioned before, the average person would only meet approximately 50 people in their entire lifetime. The main purpose of coupling up was that both men and women needed to reproduce, it was the prime motivator of the relationship. They would however already work as a partnership. The man would go and kill the buffalo, provide security, whilst the woman would forage and look after the children.

It was actually only in Victorian times that the notion of romantic attachment became an essential part of marriage. Things have changed enormously over the last century, with some countries now allowing gay marriages. In the western world, the notion of love is now the basis of any long term relationship and the focus is no longer survival. Since World War 2, and through socio-economic advances, most of us now seek comfort and quality of life.

With the internet and advent of social media, we have a very different outlook and always seem to want more. All of this has made us fussier, as we unconsciously seek perfection in all aspects of our lives, from the material aspects to careers, and obviously in our relationships. We don't all want a Ferrari for instance and some of us will only want a simple life. However, we will have an idea of what it represents. It is actually a concept very personal to each and every single one of us. What is perfection anyway? Once we understand ourselves, we are more likely to understand what is truly important within. Accepting another person for who they are without trying to change them is essential, and we should love their good points as well as their 'flaws'. A perfect relationship is when both parties are there to complement each other. Both look at life in the same way and head in the same direction, whilst remaining true to themselves.

The key is also real communication. Again, we know that but we forget. It is often one of the first things that goes when it starts to go wrong, along with sex. Actually, sexual intimacy is another way of communicating our feelings towards each other. People often feel that they haven't got a communication issue because they talk about lots of 'stuff'. Mundane and routine subjects don't count I'm afraid to say. I actually recall overhearing a conversation once, where the lady was telling her friend that she'd been out for dinner with her husband the night before, but because there were no kids to disturb them, they had nothing to talk about. That's really sad. True communication is about our feelings, emotions or inner thoughts, and these need to be spoken about regularly. A touch or a kiss are also simple ways to express the way we feel and bring a sense of reassurance.

Ask anyone currently going through the dating process and most of them will admit to having a 'type'. There are certain physical and mental traits that we actively and consciously seek in a partner. What people often don't realise is that we also go for other elements of someone's personality, but on an unconscious level.

In fact, once again, this is because the relationships that we attract and choose to have are actually the direct reflection of the relationship we have with ourselves. For instance, someone struggling with their own self-worth will most probably attract those who will not make them feel so good about themselves. That person will unconsciously look for their partner to fill that gap and satisfy that need, where really, they are the only ones who can address the issue and will need to look within.

In the same way that you shouldn't want to change someone to fit what you would want them to be, you are only responsible for yourself. Any change that you wish to go through will have to come from you. Nobody can make you happy or complete you, you complete yourself. Realising that, and more importantly accepting it, is probably the most important step forward to finding the right person for you.

We don't often allow ourselves to question our deepest needs and address them. We also sometimes need a little help in recognising what exactly it is we are all about, or want, before we can acknowledge and change our habits. It sounds a bit mad really because we all think we know what we want, but very few of us really do. This is why for instance, a lot of people in settled relationships are often the first ones to be surprised as their partner is so different from what they were originally looking for. It is important to reflect on what you need to learn about yourself in order to stop making the mistakes of the past.

People often repeat the same patterns of behaviours relationship after relationship, wondering why things don't work out. A close friend of mine did exactly that, and it has taken him 12 years to realise that the reason is purely himself. He was The Ostrich. Up to that point, he would explain the fact he couldn't have a fulfilling relationship with grand theories on timing and that he deserved better. He generally blamed the world and everyone else. We worked together and once he was actually honest with himself, accepting that the reasons were always the same and down to him, he realised he had a choice. It dawned on him that he was the only person that could remedy that and started to work on himself. His problem was that he didn't let anyone know about how he really felt. He was scared it would upset the balance.

It is sometimes difficult to assess what we do 'wrong' and how we could improve. No-one likes to point the finger at themselves. This isn't about being overly critical about yourself in an unhelpful manner. It's about asking the right questions. For example, if one of your main complaints is that you attract people who neglect you, ask yourself how you could be more attentive to your own needs instead of wanting someone else to do it for you. One of the secrets to long lasting relationships is to know yourself and be happy in your own company, only looking to someone else to add to your life as opposed to expecting them to complete it.

I am regularly asked if the flame can be re-ignited with an ex-partner. The upshot of it is basically that it depends but it's surprising how we sometimes still hold a bit of a torch, or just always had a soft spot for a certain person. Some partners actually touch our hearts in a different way and leave a longer lasting mark. When we look back, our mind can wonder about what would have been or question why the relationship really ended. Maybe that person is even the one regret you have because you let them go. There is a particular sentimental element about this and as we reflect, thinking about our time together, our heart swells and fills with warmth. This is often the case if the split wasn't clear-cut, as it is more difficult to get closure.

Sometimes, relationships end because the time is just not quite right. Sometimes, because both people are on different journeys and have to go through separate life experiences. And then one day, after years apart, life throws a bit of synchronicity your way, and you meet again or your circumstances change. Either way, it's causing you to question things. That little niggly something between you two is still there…

So what should you do? Should you both explore your feelings again? Is it really a good idea? After all, it didn't work the first time around so it surely is a recipe for disaster? Again, every situation is different and needs to be assessed on its own merits. Just remember that we all change and grow as we go through life. We all get through different experiences, which mould us maybe in a different way. Very few people could argue they are the same person today than they were 10 or 15 years ago. I know I'm certainly not. So the question is, have you both evolved in the same way or towards the same life purpose? After all, it could just be that the timing was off when you first met, and that you are now ready for each other. And there really is only one way to find out, which is to talk openly about it. The key here is honest communication and remaining true to who you are **now**.

Meeting someone from the past can sometimes take you back to the person you were with them (for a short while) as opposed to the person you have become. As both will have changed, you will be getting to know each other again in the same way as you would with someone new. The only real difference is that you have a bit of a past together and some shared memories. In this circumstance, because we already know the person, we feel a certain sense of security and comfort which is a form of reassurance in a way. For those reasons, there may be higher expectations and you should be mindful of that. The feelings of disappointment and hurt can both be exacerbated if things don't work out this time.

So… should you? Well ultimately, it's up to you but life threw you back together for a reason so as long as you are both on the same page, why not find out? After all, whether it works or not, maybe it is better to know rather than to live life with regrets or questions. It could just be that the chapter needed to be closed and a lesson learnt from it all. It could also just be that you weren't ready for each other before but have now grown to be perfect together. If the flame can be re-ignited, it was never totally extinguished.

Either way and whether you are single, dating, in a relationship or married for years, remember to stop comparing your situation with other people's. This is particularly true in today's world, and mainly fuelled by social media. We have discussed this but it's an essential part of fixing the relationship you have with yourself. Always remember that people are very good at creating the perception of the perfect life that you would want. They seem to have it all and it makes you feel inadequate or like you're missing out. When you feel down, it makes you unconsciously question your life and levels of happiness. From where you are looking in, they have it all and you wish you did. It's very easy to get wrapped in the negative downward spiral instead. How many times have you actually found out and been surprised to hear that a happy couple isn't getting on as well as you thought? People put on a front. Not just for you to envy them, but because they don't want to confront their own issues. You know this because you now have the tools to be different to them. We create our own reality, remember... And even if they are genuinely happy, they are not you and you are not them. So what's right and works for them wouldn't work for you, and vice versa. On a daily basis, remind yourself of all the good things that you have and be grateful for them. Always thinking about what's wrong and focusing on the negative will only make things worse.

Always trust your gut instinct, this is the most important thing. We all know deep down what we need to do and what the state of affairs really is. Go with what feels good, because the gut really is the second brain. You should always take into consideration what it tells you because it will always be right. The logical and rational side of the brain that tell you what you should or ought to do unfortunately can't be trusted. In my opinion, you should only make decisions based on how you feel.

You need to be aware that as a result of this journey of self-discovery, the outcome may not be what you thought it would be when you started this book. You know what's wrong and you already know what needs to be addressed. Your higher self also knows how to remedy it. We have all the resources we need, remember? Be The Tiger, not The Ostrich. Listen to what Your Other Half has to say instead of being left wondering why you're so unhappy. Be honest with yourself and don't force anything. Let go and allow a perfect flow into your life. You may realise that your relationship is actually dead and that you need to walk away. Remember that people come and go into our lives, mainly to develop us and make us grow. It's also about recognising that sometimes, we are no longer a perfect match because we have evolved in different directions. Having the inner strength and courage to walk away is the right thing to do in that case. If it no longer serves you, it no longer serves the other person either. But if it's not too late, then do the work together. If you both want to save a troubled relationship, you will.

If you are single, take a bit of time out to work your way through the process, then start again. Very soon, the relationship that you have with yourself will be a very positive one. As a result, everything will fall into place. You are in charge of your mind and therefore, of your own results. Have faith and trust in the process. You have come across this book for a reason and it will help you shift in your awareness. Little point in asking why, just concentrate on the solution.

So does the perfect relationship exist? Yes, if we create it as what we want it to be. It is something very personal to two individuals and only they'll understand it. Everybody else will have their own opinions, so dismiss other people's view of perfection. If it feels right, it will be right so stick to what you believe it to be. It's just a perception anyway…

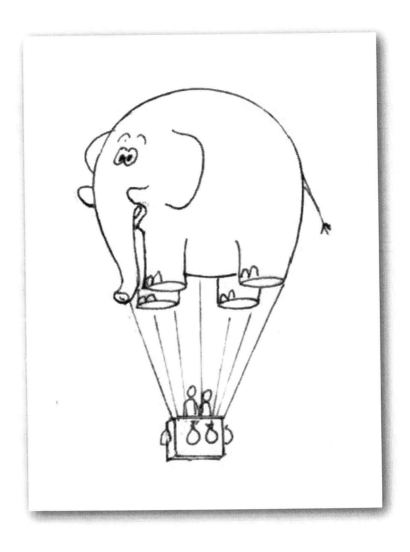

About The Author

Sophie was born in France and moved to the UK in 1999. She studied 'International Relations & Politics' at Portsmouth University and her early career was in the security industry. She started working for herself after taking redundancy in 2012 and hasn't looked back.

After setting up an events company designed for single professionals, Sophie realised that most of the attendees actually weren't psychologically ready to be dating or with very unrealistic expectations. This was the point where she felt it would be far more productive to help them on their journey. Along the way, she started to attract people with different types of relationship issues, such as marriage problems or difficulties with family members, as well as people battling their own personal struggles.

Sophie found in her previous working life that most people would at some point come to her for advice. Being the only woman in an environment full of testosterone provided a real insight into the male psyche and taught her invaluable lessons.

Training in NLP, and especially putting all the concepts into practice, changed her life. She feels very privileged to have worked with many different people over the years, each and every one of them as well as their own experiences, contributing to her wealth of knowledge and understanding.

Her aim is to inspire and improve people's lives. If you want to know more, you can visit her website **www.sophiepersonne.com**.

Printed in Great Britain
by Amazon